Advance Praise for *Communicating Under Fire*

"Lawrence has written a punchy and pragmatic guide to understanding and navigating crises effectively. His book is stacked full of enlightening examples and colorful stories that bring his recommendations to life with verve and specificity."

–Tim Cadogan, CEO of Go Fund Me

"Dallas Lawrence provides the mindset anyone with a reputation worth defending needs to not only survive their crisis moment, but thrive through it."

–Dr. Allison Barber, President
and Chief Operating Officer,
Indiana Fever WNBA Franchise

COMMUNICATING

THE MINDSET TO SURVIVE ANY CRISIS

UNDER

AND EMERGE STRONGER

FIRE

DALLAS LAWRENCE

Post Hill
PRESS

A POST HILL PRESS BOOK
ISBN: 979-8-88845-561-6
ISBN (eBook): 979-8-88845-562-3

Communicating Under Fire:
The Mindset to Survive Any Crisis and Emerge Stronger
© 2024 by Dallas Lawrence
All Rights Reserved

Cover design by Conroy Accord

Post Hill Press
New York • Nashville
posthillpress.com

Published in the United States of America
1 2 3 4 5 6 7 8 9 10

To my incredible wife Sarah and our amazing kids Emma, Abby, and Christopher for supporting me during so many crazy crisis rollercoaster rides. With your love, no crisis has ever seemed insurmountable.

TABLE OF CONTENTS

INTRODUCTION

On October 6, 2021, a tweet sent by a senior-level engineer at Netflix, the world's largest streaming service, went viral, and in the process, provided one of the clearest examples for how fundamentally the crisis management game has changed in today's modern, digitally connected world. The tweet and its aftermath would challenge corporate crisis doctrine, test the power of celebrity and creative freedom, and frame for the world the very clear reality that today anyone, at any time, can cause immediate and significant reputational harm to an organization.

Terra Field, a transgender Netflix employee and co-vice president of Netflix's Trans Employee Resource Group, took to the platform now known as X (which, at the time in the pre-Elon Musk era, was still known as Twitter), to share her concerns about a new Dave Chappelle special featuring derogatory comments about the transgender and LGBTQ community. Comedy specials are no laughing matter for the streamer; Netflix has placed a great deal of focus on its commitment to comedy, and to Chapelle in particular. In 2021, the comedian ranked as the most watched ever for Netflix. But with a single tweet, Field ignited a crisis wildfire that brought together nearly every element fueling reputational challenges in the early 2020s—cancel culture, changing employee expectations for inclusive policies and their desire to see their organizations take political stands, hyper-charged social media driven by professional advocacy groups, and a traditional media that is so hungry for eyeballs it is willing to wade with breathless speed into nearly every sensational ratings-driven moment.

In response to Field's tweet, Netflix also committed many of the classic missteps that have plagued so many organizations in the past decade: a rush to engage, a tone-deaf reaction, a misread of the landscape, and ultimately the need to change course entirely. Netflix co-CEO Ted Sarandos, who unwittingly became the center of the fire and its chief source of fuel, was himself an unapologetic fan of Chappelle. In a memo to Netflix employees, Sarandos defended Chapelle's new show as a work of "creative freedom," saying they would not take it down. For many observers who watched the Netflix tale unfold, it was a wakeup call. Entertainment leaders were initially caught off-guard by the harsh reaction to what many viewed as a CEO standing by his creative talent. Instead of being championed for it, Sarandos was being taken to the woodshed. What only a few short years ago would have been heralded as a courageous stance for artistic integrity was now Exhibit A for how entertainment companies were propelling transphobia.

Netflix's employees planned a walkout while talent and creative leaders threatened to boycott working for the company altogether. It was becoming, in the parlance of crisis communicators, a classic example of "breaking into jail." The crisis fire never needed to burn this hot had Netflix, and its CEO, not so dramatically misread the situation and unwittingly fanned the flames.

While the situation unfolding for the Netflix team likely seemed it would never leave the headlines, it only took seventy-two hours for another fire to erupt in an entirely different corporate boardroom that would shake consumer confidence and rattle stock valuations.

On October 9, the crisis that would ensnare a beloved airline further highlighted the evolving traps facing anyone with a reputation worth defending. On this particular Saturday morning, thousands of travelers awoke to the news that their Southwest Airlines flights had been canceled.

As stressed-out passengers flooded call centers and customer service lines at the airport frantic to get home, the news only got worse when they learned that all flights had just been canceled for the next several days. Flight delays and even mass cancellations were not unheard of as America and the world still struggled to emerge from the age of COVID-19 precautions. Southwest clearly had a well-worn plan for communicating with customers during largescale disruptions. Nonetheless, as with Netflix, what could have been a managed moment in time for the brand, unfortunately became a headline-ringing crisis, dragging the airline into a cultural battle involving nearly every dark corner of the modern professional outrage machine.

While Southwest claimed the cancellations were weather related, the issue was quickly commandeered to America's brewing civil war over vaccinations. Just days earlier, Southwest had announced that all employees needed to be vaccinated against the COVID-19 virus. Conservative social media users and reporters seized on the opportunity to tie the unrelated events together, leveraging Southwest's relative silence during the weekend cancellations with a newly spun explanation that pilots and other Southwest staff must be calling in sick to protest the vaccine mandate. Southwest's plan for managing flight cancellations due to weather was developed for a different age and left the airline exposed and unprepared for the storm blowing in from the far reaches of the post-truth world.

Three days after the initial crisis began for Southwest—a lifetime in today's 1440 news cycle, where every one of the 1440 minutes in a day can impact a reputation—the company finally released a statement apologizing and explaining the delays. The explanation was simple: Weather and "air traffic constraints" led to cancellations at Orlando International Airport, Southwest's largest connection point, which cascaded across the country and impacted the entire airline's operations. Southwest's president and COO, Mike Van de Ven, insisted that the cancellations had nothing to do with any "unusual" employee activity.

Unfortunately for Van de Ven, his explanation and the airline's overall response was simply too little, too late. Conservative and liberal news outlets alike connected the two events together in countless articles. Matters became even more challenging when hundreds of current and former Southwest employees gathered at the company's headquarters in Texas to protest the vaccine mandate, a protest organized by the very same groups that had initially spun the false narrative about Southwest to breathe further oxygen onto the fire.

During one week in 2021, two of the biggest and most influential companies in America, both with passionate customer bases and a history of successfully navigating the crisis waters, stumbled badly in the court of public opinion. In both Netflix's and Southwest's cases, there was nothing either could have done to avoid their own corporate crisis from initially occurring. Controversy is going to come your way when you invest $14 billion annually in new content, and weather delays are bound to happen for airlines flying hundreds of routes every day. In each case, however, and in the case of nearly every major reputational challenge faced by organizations and individuals in the past two decades, it was what they did (or did not do) next after their crisis emerged that determined their eventual fate.

Our World in Crisis

The 2020s seem to be engulfed in an almost never-ending cycle of crisis, with Netflix and Southwest Airlines serving as just two prescient examples of what lies ahead. At the time of this writing, it has been nearly 4 years since protestors stormed the US Capitol. Donald Trump is on track to complete the biggest comeback in political history cruising through the Republican nomination for President. The world continues to watch with sadness the horrifying images from Ukraine as Russia's military systemically wipes out both civilian and military targets alike. At the same time, the world witnessed real courage and a powerful lesson in crisis communications from Ukraine's president that will be unpacked in later chapters. The Middle East once again slipped into a traditional pattern of conflict but this time with an unprecedented level of terrorist violence from Hamas delivering the equivalent of ten 9/11 attacks on Israel civilians and an ongoing Israel counter-offensive leaving many to ask where this all ends. Businesses continue to struggle with an anemic economic recovery and complicated inflation. Racial tensions and evolving norms around gender and sexual orientation remain top of mind for everyone from the local school board leader to the Fortune 500 executive. And of course, all these rising tension points come in the aftermath of the once-in-a-century pandemic that claimed the lives of millions that many countries are still struggling to emerge from economically and politically. From political battlefields to corporate boardroom dramas, from the individual threatened with cancel culture to the large organization facing increased pressure from employees, in the emerging post-COVID, post-Trump (for now), and post-truth world, everywhere you look there is a new crisis boiling just under the surface.

I have been in the crisis trenches for the past quarter century, yet even to me, the ever-present critical world eye feels different. Forty years ago, before the advent of the internet, when there were only a limited number of media outlets, crisis responders had a familiar playbook. Crisis managers created well thought-out plans, developed multi-ringed binders tabbed with bright colors for each likely scenario, and developed their written responses for each scenario. On occasion, the crisis teams would gather and rehearse each scenario, dutifully following the guidelines in each tabbed binder section and, after their afternoon of training, they would congratulate themselves on a well-executed exercise. With the right strategies and a seasoned hand at the wheel, the truth—or your version of it—could often win the day.

Today, when literally anyone can report breaking news faster than reporters, anyone's version of the truth can take hold and spread like wildfire. In *Trust Me, I'm Lying: Confessions of a Media Manipulator*, Ryan Holiday sums up the problem nicely: "The problem is that the truth—your response—is often much less interesting than the accusations." This is the world we live in today: a post-truth world fueled by social algorithms designed to provide a steady stream of sensational news to propel our click-bait society.

The old adage, often attributed to Mark Twain, that "a lie can travel halfway around the world while the truth is still putting its shoes on" has never been truer. Yet, even this old statement serves as a reminder for how misinformation, when repeated often enough, becomes fact. More than a hundred websites claim this quote to be from Mark Twain. The reality is he never uttered these words. While the true author remains unknown, the message remains no less true. In this environment, every leader with a reputation worth defending can, in a moment, find themselves struggling against a mountain of untrue "evidence" against them. The old playbook has outlived its usefulness.

In 2011, as social media began overhauling the world of crisis communications, I was invited to develop the crisis communications graduate course for the USC Annenberg

School of Communications. While developing course materials to teach the next generation of business leaders how to manage through a crisis in the modern digital age, I realized just how few useful books existed to help develop the *mindset* necessary for an effective crisis communications strategy. And the problem has only compounded in the years since.

Following the election of Donald Trump as America's forty-fifth president, we entered a new chapter of crisis communications, one in which every minute of the day counts. Companies that had never waded into hot button issues such as immigration or racial justice were now being pressured by their employees and their customers to take a "political stand." Media outlets were being whipsawed from one headline-driving crisis to the next. As I watched each new crisis unfold, it seemed clear that many of those working to protect reputations and manage crises were losing. My students and my clients were all asking the same question: "How do we survive a crisis in this age of instant media?"

What I found to be lacking was a practical book to help anyone with a reputation worth defending understand the risks of today's always-on, always-connected worldwide media environment.

To be sure, there are many books available today about effective crisis management. These books provide detailed crisis plans and "how-to guides" readers can attempt to follow. This is not that book. If you think of a crisis management plan like the hoses, axes, suits, and other tools firefighters use, then you might see that just because you have those tools in your garage doesn't mean you'll know how to use them safely and strategically if your house catches on fire. When a crisis breaks out today, even the best plans can fail to address the nuances and traps of social media and the fickle tides of public opinion. However, with the right knowledge, training, and mindset, you can utilize a crisis plan and adapt it with skill and effectiveness—just as experienced firefighters wield their tools. In my experience, what was missing from the current collection of resources was a practical crisis management guide centered around real-world wisdom to help anyone prepare in advance for crisis-ridden times and implement a successful crisis recovery plan quickly. That is the goal of this book.

No two crisis fires are alike, especially in today's world. However, as any seasoned firefighter will tell you, there is a natural way in which every fire burns. There is a science to it—a well-worn path it will follow again and again and again. Once learned, you can anticipate how it will move and, ultimately, how to extinguish it.

Fighting Crisis Fires

I knew the exact moment I first wanted to be a "crisis firefighter." It was on a blisteringly hot day in 2004 after I had accepted an appointment by President George W. Bush to serve as a spokesperson for the war in Iraq.

I had been "in country" for about a month, wading into the swelling crisis storm that was the Iraq war and reconstruction effort in an attempt to shape strategic media outcomes for the United States and our coalition partners. That day began like any other—just as your crisis day will.

I was twenty-eight and sitting behind the wheel of a sparkling gold, fully armored SUV, feeling every bit the confidence a single adventure-seeker would feel in the same situation. I hoped my journey to Baghdad would unlock a new chapter in my career—a career that had, up until that point, led me down a path as a press hack for various elected officials, spinning fascinating stories about farm subsidies and international trade debates on Capitol Hill. I believed that public relations could be one of the most consequential tools any business, government, or individual had at their disposal, and I wanted a bigger arena to practice my trade. In accepting the Iraq posting, I'd sought out the biggest stage possible to expand my knowledge of the craft of crisis management.

My colleagues and I were returning from a successful media event with the United States Ambassador to Iraq. Without warning, all traffic around our vehicle came to a grinding halt. It was a moment that sent our stomachs plummeting. We realized we were sitting ducks in the middle of an unmoving morass of tinted window sedans, beat-up Toyota pickup trucks, horse-drawn carts pulling vegetable stands, and hundreds of pedestrians swarming together in the cramped mosh pits that comprise Baghdad's streets.

Within moments, all outside eyes turned and fingers began pointing toward our vehicle. At this precise moment, I began reevaluating both the logic I had used to make the case for this day's trip, as well as the logic of whichever government bean-counter decided to buy bright gold-colored SUVs for us to use. We were the only people in the entire country of Iraq who drove vehicles this color. And we had a lot of them.

We could not have made for an easier target for the country's growing insurgency if we tried. Several weeks prior, a colleague's Suburban faced a similar situation, coming under fire as they returned to the safety of Baghdad's protective Green Zone cocoon from the hostile Red Zone. Insurgent fighters and radicalized followers of a few clerics were seeking every opportunity to attack the Coalition. Sitting unmoving in our bright-gold SUV made us the perfect target.

With tensions mounting, we found ourselves at the epicenter of a potential riot. His M-16 now firmly gripped, the number two gunner in our vehicle leaned forward and directed me to "Turn this car around and follow that donkey!" The donkey in question was pulling a cart down a side street in the complete opposite direction of traffic. Separating us was not only a mass of traffic and people, but a sizable cement barrier as well.

After scanning the rooftops for possible snipers or rocket-propelled grenade launchers, the colonel sitting behind me snapped, "Get us out of here!" It was an order directed at yours truly who had decided to hop behind the driver's seat for the trip that morning. With that order, the Air Force lieutenant colonel in the passenger's seat beside me clicked the safety off her nine-millimeter Beretta handgun and made it clear it was time to move. Everything next happened so quickly, it felt like I was watching it unfold in slow motion.

In a scene straight out of a Jack Ryan movie, a third soldier in the rear of the vehicle jumped out with his M-16 drawn and began creating a hole in the traffic for me to pierce through. I recall to this day the complete lack of hesitation he showed in jumping out of the armored vehicle to create room for our vehicle to move. With lookouts watching the roof lines and our "traffic cop" moving cars one by one at the point of a gun, I managed to turn the glittering eight-passenger behemoth around into oncoming traffic. The vehicle jumped into action as I hit the accelerator, with the V8 engine roaring to life. As I dodged and weaved through the oncoming cars in the middle of rush hour, my orders were clear: I was looking for just the right moment when the cement median barrier subsided enough to jump "Dukes of Hazard-style" over the center divider and careen through four lanes of traffic to reach the donkey going down a side alley. With adrenaline pumping, the moment came to pull the wheel to jump the barrier. As our 5,000-pound vehicle momentarily achieved flight, my only thought was of finding that donkey. *Where the fuck was it?* I had lost it in the rush of dodging traffic and jumping curbs.

Thankfully, seconds after hitting the ground, I found him again. With a few screeching turns, I managed to cross multiple lanes of traffic to safety. I was pushing the maximum speed limit of our armored vehicle, my passengers' guns drawn in a defensive posture, and I had just broken about every traffic law imaginable.

We careened through the street and into the donkey's alley. Finally away from the crowds, the lieutenant colonel leaned over, placed a hand on my shoulder, and said "We've made it." I had an almost out-of-body experience, from both the release as well as the need to stay focused on every detail in front of me, yet strangely I also felt a sense of calm and focus.

It was not just being in a war zone or the possible risk of losing my life that gave me the rush of adrenaline—it was the realization that my work had purpose. My immediate actions, what I did next, and what I did after that, determined the success or failure of our efforts to successfully navigate that unforeseen situation.

In any crisis, whether in a literal combat zone or a virtual battlefield, there are a thousand opportunities to fail. And, as you'll see in many of the stories throughout this book, while lives may not always be on the line, reputations will be. That experience, and the realization it provided me would forever alter the course of my career.

Two decades later, while Iraq stands as my only active combat zone assignment, my work in the crisis communications world has taken me to Yemen in an effort to avert the Yemini civil war, to the Guantanamo Bay terrorist detention facilities in Cuba, and to the Horn of Africa's command center for anti-pirating activities. I've helped manage crisis media responses for nuclear disasters, celebrity scandals, the Boston terror bombing, the collapse of Wall Street, the Boy Scout sexual assault crisis, data breaches, COVID-19 responses, and cancel culture. I've included many of these stories in the pages of this book. The instincts and experiences gained from these "front-row seats" have profoundly shaped my approach to the science behind crisis management today.

The Path Forward

My hope is that this book prepares you for this one inevitable truth: It is simply a matter of when, not if, your crisis moment will occur. My goal in this book is to help prepare anyone with a reputation worth defending to not only survive a crisis moment in the spotlight, but hopefully to emerge positioned to thrive.

In Part I: Preparing During Peacetime, we'll dive deeper into understanding the nuances of today's media landscape and how to use your "peacetime" productively. You'll be able to pivot, adjust, and stay agile much more easily in the throes of a crisis if you have a working knowledge of the landscape and take the right actions to prepare.

In Part II: Responding to a Crisis, we will walk through each moment of your crisis—when the traffic suddenly stops, and you find that what just moments ago was a routine day has turned into a public relations nightmare. For most of us, our natural human instincts of fight, flight, or freeze will ultimately make matters worse. Staying calm and decisive will be critically important in this phase when others are controlling the narrative. You'll learn about the different response options you have, and how to use them to stop the damage from spreading. These proactive strategies will help turn the tide of public opinion so that *you* can regain control of the narrative and, if you seize the right opportunities, perhaps even emerge from the crisis better than you were before.

When the time comes and a crisis moment is upon you, the path forward isn't a dark and unknown one. There is a science to how crisis fires burn, and *Communicating Under Fire* will take you on that journey through the fire to discover how to protect, defend, and ultimately rebuild a reputation while under fire.

PART I

Preparing During Peacetime

W hile it is true that there is no way to avoid all possible crises, there is plenty you can do to prepare for when your crisis moment comes. Leaders who are well-equipped to manage crises have an understanding, and an appreciation for, the rapidly evolving media world in which we all now live. In Part I, we will delve into some of the most intense and highly publicized crises of the last twenty years, dissecting the right and wrong steps many organizations and individuals have taken. For those who faltered during these moments, the usual culprit is a false sense of the "It could never happen to us" syndrome. Crisis victims believe in the golden days of their peacetimes, instead of using the peacetime to prepare wisely for the inevitable future. On the flip side, those who have survived and recovered from a crisis have witnessed the PR nightmares faced by others and thought, "There, but for the grace of God, go I" and prepared accordingly.

In my years as a crisis manager, I have learned that there are several steps anyone with a reputation worth preserving can take while things are going well. When your fire alarm moment arrives, you'll be grateful you invested in the knowledge, people, and procedures that ultimately prove to be your saving grace.

CHAPTER 1

WHEN, NOT IF

"There cannot be a crisis next week.
My schedule is already full."

-Henry Kissinger

n September 2008, United Airlines was finally enjoying some good times. The company was on the rebound from recent bankruptcy proceedings and was beginning to move past its restructuring woes. Leadership was able to focus on the future. Things seemed to be flying high once again.

On the morning of September 8, hundreds of United flights were in the air. But by mid-morning, everything came crashing down. At 11:00 a.m., the company's stock plummeted 99 percent—hitting a valuation of just one penny per share before an emergency trading halt was triggered at 11:08 a.m.

Had a plane crashed? Was United back in bankruptcy? The financial markets and traders hastily tried to make sense of the chaos. They weren't alone. Even United's executives were in the dark—clueless as to why the stock of the company they had spent so many years trying to rebuild had been, in mere seconds, rendered next to worthless.

As the minutes turned to hours, pieces of the puzzle began coming into view. *The New York Times* strung together the chain of events that ultimately ignited the stock crash, writing: "Shares of United Airlines lost nearly all their value Monday morning when a false rumor swept financial markets that the struggling carrier had filed for bankruptcy protection…. In a statement, United said the rumor occurred when the website of *The Sun-Sentinel*, a Florida newspaper, posted a six-year-old story from *The Chicago Tribune* archives about United's previous bankruptcy filing…"

But even that story wasn't quite right. It was not *The Sun-Sentinel*'s fault; they hadn't "posted" anything. During the late evening hours of Sunday, September 7, *The Sun-Sentinel* began a routine process of archiving old news stories on their website. This involved moving stories off of the primary site into an archival section, which also removed the prominent dateline placements of the stories. Because of how stories were moved within their web architecture, the process triggered Google News alerts for certain keywords. And now a years-old article looked like breaking news.

That might not have mattered, but sometime in the early morning hours of Monday, September 8, an enterprising writer working for Income Securities Advisors, a Miami-based investment research firm, came across the article in his newsfeed while searching for information about bankruptcies. Thinking he would be the first to push a blockbuster story out to his Wall Street trader audience, the writer quickly posted an article to Bloomberg News based on the old report. Suddenly, it was on the desktops of thousands of traders, who quickly dumped their shares. And before you could say, "The captain has turned the seat belt sign on," billions of dollars in valuation were—temporarily—wiped off the map as United's stock trading ground to a halt. It was through no fault of the airline or malice by the article's author. Just a questionable algorithm, quick reading, and hasty trading.

By that afternoon, the facts were cleared up and the stock resumed trading. But the damage was done. United's stock still closed down 10 percent for the day, dragged down by a market that had been forced to relive—in the most startling circumstances—the airline's past financial struggles.

"So, how do you avoid a crisis?"

It's the question I get asked most often in the crisis communications business. It is a natural question, and it's not a bad starting point. But it can't be the only question you ask. Because here's the reality that I always have to break to people, including some of the world's top CEOs: It's not a question of *if* you'll face a crisis. It is a question of *when*. In 2021, the public relations firm Edelman published the findings of a crisis survey of executives that further accentuates the inevitability of crises. Eighty-eight percent of executives surveyed reported that their business had faced at least one large-scale crisis that impacted their bottom lines in the past thirty-six months.

Organizations spend millions of dollars and endless hours on risk management and mitigation teams. They assess every possible threat and develop measures to prevent those threats. I will never forget working with a major oil and gas company to develop their crisis plan. The company had a 200-page binder, with tabs color-coded by topic, assessing every possible crisis scenario the company could face and what they had done to mitigate that crisis from occurring. Yet, when I turned to the section in this perfectly tabbed binder about how to respond to a crisis publicly, the page simply read, "Contact PR team." Unfortunately, most organizations, even some of the most powerful corporations on earth, spend very little time—if any—on actually preparing for the inevitable: when "it" hits the fan.

And, again, it *will* hit the fan.

It would be easy to chalk this oversight up to executive wishful thinking—leaders simply not believing a crisis will impact *their* business. But nearly all available data points in the opposite direction. A 2014 survey of businesses executives found that 78 percent, nearly eight out of ten, believed their business was less than twelve months away from experiencing a serious crisis. More than half also believed that the crisis would be perpetuated in the digital space, filled with a dizzying array of social media platforms, millions of potential bloggers and other social influencers, each with a potential axe to grind and all with the potential to wreak havoc on a reputation. Less than a decade later, the Edelman survey found the current state of readiness had actually worsened in the face of so many headline crisis moments. More than three out of four executives believe their organizations will face another significant crisis in the next thirty-six months. Less than half of those surveyed believe they are well-prepared for when the moment comes.

Despite this level of self-awareness, many are doing nothing about it. Fully one-third of companies lack a crisis management plan today, and nearly half of executives in one survey admit they do not even have a basic form of effective online reputation monitoring. Not only are these organizations and leaders not prepared for a crisis, many don't even have the most rudimentary tools to know if their reputations are under assault. This would be like knowing for certain your house is going to be robbed, and yet not even asking a neighbor to keep an eye on things, never mind installing a security system.

The scenario we face today is truly a perfect reputational storm—and it is one that faces the corporate boardroom, the family business, the non-profit, the local school principal, media celebrity and government entities alike. Ownership of crisis response is murky, few have a basic plan, and most have no tools for threat detection.

So, returning to the opening story of this chapter, we ask ourselves if there is anything United could have done to avoid their crisis moment. Again, we find the answer is no. United's number had simply been called. A crisis team's responsibility is therefore to be ready for the inevitable. Had United set up a rapid-response monitoring program and immediately shared findings with their crisis response teams (assuming these teams were operating), they would have captured in real time the news report and been able to mitigate the damage. As it was, United would not launch its Twitter account, a powerful rapid response tool that will be discussed in later chapters, for another year. What was clear from United's initial response was that they had not linked together teams and capabilities designed to detect and correct reputational risks in real time. In United's case, there was no malice, no employee acting poorly, nor was there a hacker working to bring down the grid. A falsehood accidently slipped into the airstream and traveled halfway around the world before United was able to get its shoes on.

If this book achieves only one thing, hopefully it is to raise awareness that it is simply a matter of when, not if, your moment in the harsh spotlight will come. How you prepare for crisis during "peacetime" will determine your likelihood of surviving it—or perhaps even emerging victorious from it.

In other words, crisis *prevention* is a nice idea. But equal, if not more, effort should be expended on crisis *preparation and response*. Those who have found the quickest path out of turbulence and back to smoother sailing are those who had already accepted, embraced even, the inevitability of facing a crisis moment and made the investments to plan, train, and develop the reflexes to spring into action.

Accepting this reality will ensure you and your teams are as prepared as possible when your number is called. The following chapters in this book will lay out the right questions to ask before a crisis, the necessary steps needed to prepare for when it comes, and the proven insights to successfully navigate through the crisis waters.

CHAPTER 2
THE 1440 NEWS CYCLE

"It takes 20 years to build a reputation and five minutes to ruin it."

–Warren Buffett

I n the 1970s, TV news was dominated by three broadcast networks: ABC, NBC, and CBS. All that changed on June 1, 1980, when the Cable News Network (CNN) splashed onto the scene, marrying the power of satellite and cable to provide everyone in the country access to the same information around the clock. Suddenly, news became more like sports, with new developments unfolding before viewers' eyes, sparking a hunger for something no one even knew was possible. It was the beginning of the end for the morning paper and the evening news. By being first to cover critical events like the Challenger explosion and the Gulf War, CNN set the bar for immediate news coverage. And by the 1990s, the constant refrain in the crisis business was to be ever vigilant managing the "24/7 news cycle."

Yet even as the speed of change in the media landscape advanced at a dizzying pace through the first decade of the 2000s, the basic rules of media engagement remained largely the same. A small(ish) set of key reporters and news outlets still defined much of what was considered to be news.

The field of media would again undergo a sea-change moment in 2006. Facebook had begun its expansion outside of college campuses and Twitter roared onto the scene, allowing for rapid-fire updates to flood unfiltered into the marketplace. Within a year, the iPhone would put those updates in people's pockets, forever changing how, when, and where the public consumed news and information.

It was at about this time that I gave my first speech on the end of the 24/7 news cycle and the emergence of the 1440 news cycle—one in which literally every minute in a day counts during a crisis. When you consider all that happens in just sixty seconds today, you begin to understand the importance of each one of those 1,440 minutes. Each minute, tens of millions of tweets, YouTube videos, Reddit posts, Facebook updates, Snaps, Instagrams, blogs, and TikToks are posted. Each one of these has the power to light a crisis fire that will be impossible to extinguish without good preparation and constant readiness.

This tsunami of content has so overwhelmed most risk managers today that many have simply chosen to tune out the online dialogue, waiting for the crisis to transition into what for them remains the "real world" of old media.

The reality is that for most crises today, the line between the online and the offline world has blurred beyond recognition. This blurring took center stage during the biggest terrorist attack in America since 9/11. What resulted was the first manhunt ever to be covered live in the 1440 news cycle, and I had a front-row seat to see how this moment would forever change crisis relations.

Lessons from the First Live-Coverage Manhunt

On Patriot's Day 2013, thousands of spectators stood in Copley Square, cheering on as runners crossed the finish line of the 117th Boston Marathon. Many reported that the day was cool and sunny; a beautiful day that no one suspected would turn deadly merely five hours after the start of the race. But at 2:49 p.m., brothers Tamerlan and Dzhokhar Tsarnaev detonated two homemade bombs, tearing into the crowd near the finish line.

Three individuals were killed, and hundreds were injured, setting off one of the most watched manhunts in the history of the new media era. From the outset, it was clear that this crisis would be covered differently by the media. Within minutes of the explosions, video footage and still photographs began appearing online from witnesses, and the Boston Police Department began collecting the footage, piecing together the groundwork for their investigation. On CNN, news anchor Anderson Cooper checked his Twitter feed live on air, reporting updates in real time.

In the immediate aftermath of the bombing, I received a call from Boston Police Commissioner Edward Davis's office. A giant of a man, Commissioner Davis was old school Boston police, the kind of man who made you feel safer knowing he was leading one of the most respected police forces in America. Several months earlier, I had delivered a crisis presentation in Boston to an audience that included Commissioner Davis. During our conversation after the presentation, it was clear that he understood the changing landscape in which his department was now operating. His instincts would serve the people of Boston well during the terrorist manhunt that ensued in the days following the bombing.

In years past, the media would have settled for a once or twice daily press conference, asking their questions in a frenzied flurry and then scurrying off to file their stories. In today's 1440 news cycle, however, infrequent engagements create far too much time between updates, allowing for misinformation to creep in, for rumors to take hold, and for potentially dangerous false facts to take on shades of truth. Following the Boston bombing, the media was hungry and it needed to be fed. Amateur sleuths on Reddit, 4chan, and Twitter joined the investigation, publicly discussing possible suspects and pouring over video evidence. Rumors about the bombers spread quickly, making their way onto live television as anchors desperate for updates relaxed, or outright abandoned their vetting procedures.

Recognizing that the narrative was out of control and that false reports could potentially jeopardize the investigation, Commissioner Davis's public information team needed to develop a series of rapid-fire best practices to keep the media and the world informed as to the progress of the manhunt. Just about every media outlet on the planet was covering each new development and rumor. We sprang into action and reset the benchmark for public engagement during a criminal investigation launching the Boston Police Department into the middle of the social conversation.

Two days after the Boston bombings, CNN incorrectly reported that an arrest had been made. After the story appeared at 1:46 p.m. and was posted to their Twitter account, tens of thousands of social media posts latched on, re-tweeting and sharing the news of the arrest. Word was spread further through cable news broadcasts. It was clear that Twitter would be the medium in which this crisis story was told.

The Boston Police Department Twitter handle (@Boston_Police) quickly posted a tweet, correcting the media's claims. The tweet generated more than 10,000 shares on Twitter, ensuring that the mistaken arrest report lost steam. The episode established the BPD's social media channels as the go-to source for authoritative information and transformed media coverage of the bombing investigation from that point forward. The message was clear: If there was news to share, we would not wait for a press conference. It would be fed in real time via Twitter.

At the same time, the constant coverage of police activity by the media was inadvertently aiding the terror suspects in their efforts to avoid capture. During the search for the Tsarnaev brothers, Boston police again turned to social media to request that the public "not compromise officer safety by broadcasting live video of officers while approaching search locations." Almost instantly, major media outlets from MSNBC to Fox News began admonishing their on-air guests to avoid mentioning specific details of the hunt.

After five days, BPD's Twitter account was the first to break the news that police had apprehended Dzhokhar Tsarnaev after his brother Tamerlan was killed in a shoot-out with police. In a foreshadowing of social media's future profound role shaping traditional media coverage, BPD's tweet announcing the apprehension stating: "CAPTURED!!! The hunt is over. The search is done. The terror is over. And justice has won. Those last three words would soon find their way into the lead Associated Press headline crossing the wires declaring in bold type for all to see: "Justice Has Won."

Several weeks after the arrest was made, my former Bush administration colleague, Homeland Security Secretary Michael Chertoff, and I penned a column for the *Wall Street Journal* entitled "Terror in the Age of Twitter." I'll share this one piece from our column because it highlights, on a truly massive scale, the power of smart, strategic communications efforts to not only respond to crisis incoming fire, but to ultimately put out the fire entirely:

> One of the most remarkable aspects of the bombing investigation was the way that law enforcement employed social media to actually aid the investigation, not merely to manage the news and inform the public. Moments after photos and video of the

Boston Marathon bombing suspects were posted to FBI.gov, the government's website nearly crashed from the crush of visitors. BPD posted all of the official photos and video to social media to compensate for the lagging website and to encourage their online distribution. Many people shared these posts online—with some posts re-tweeted 16,000 to 17,000 times. Each one of these "shares" on social media increased the visibility of the pictures and video that were key to identifying and locating the suspects—and to letting the suspects know that their images were everywhere. That knowledge is likely what prompted the Tsarnaev brothers to bolt from hiding.

The Imperative of Real-Time Communication

While, thankfully, few will ever have to deal with the intensity of a terrorist manhunt, the lessons learned from Boston have had a profound impact on how we manage crises today. The intense competition to be first, to make news, and to grab attention with sensational coverage has trumped good fact-checking and the basic tenets of journalism on many occasions.

Reporters, social media commentators, and the billions of connected eyeballs online today will not wait patiently on anyone's timing to discuss an emerging crisis. Information vacuums invite rumor. Scarcity breeds concern.

Britain's Royal Family and their disastrous handling of Catherine, Princess of Wales' prolonged absence from the public eye in 2024 provides a powerful final reminder of the ferocity of today's modern media. For several months, the mother of the heir to the British throne had been absent from public view following a hastily announced medical procedure in late 2023. The typical heightened state of media interest in the Royals exploded into an all-out assault following the official release of a doctored family photo appearing to show the Princess of Wales with her three children. Online sleuths quickly debunked the validity of the photo, spinning conspiracy theorists to near comical levels.

Rather than lean in and engage with information that could calm the swirling waters, the Royal message minders went silent, empowering a conspiratorial feeding frenzy to go into overdrive. News headlines clamored for "transparency", late night talk show hosts roasted the family, even the Dublin Airport got in on the viral nature of the moment posting an obviously photoshopped image of hometown hero Cillian Murphy leaning out of a plane window with the caption, "Our new social media intern Kate did a great job capturing Cillian Murphy's return to Dublin Airport this morning after his Oscars success."

Princess Kate would ultimately share the truth with the public: she had been recovering from cancer surgery. The botched photo fiasco followed by the failure to engage ignited a moment that, rather than unite the country in support of its popular Princess, exposed the family's ongoing lack of transparency with the public. The reputational fall out will have lasting implications as many media outlets announced they would no longer accept updates from the Royal Family as officially vetted news sources. The moral of the story here is to avoid the information vacuum—it can really suck.

Turning back to Boston, we see clearly that by establishing clear lines of communication with regular updates that controlled rather than exacerbated the media frenzy, the Boston Police Department managed to balance public information needs with those of the criminal investigators. BPD established a precedent by rapidly sharing breaking news with everyone via Twitter. The transparency and access built trust with the media and opened a line of communication that not only helped inform the public but ultimately helped lead to the capture of the terror suspects.

The instinct to stay quiet, to freeze, to hope that "this too shall pass" can be tempting. In a crisis, everyone will have an opinion. The legal team will caution against saying anything. The sales team will urge communication with their customers. The investors and other stakeholders will seek answers and the media will demand immediate access. When every minute counts, the worst thing one can do in a crisis is allow others to tell the story.

CHAPTER 3

IF YOU ARE NOT LISTENING, YOU CANNOT HEAR

"Your brand is what people say about you when you're not in the room."

–Jeff Bezos, Founder and
Executive Chair, Amazon

I t goes without saying that in today's media environment, the importance of monitoring your reputation, both online and off, is paramount. Despite this reality, far too few organizations today actively monitor the conversations about them online. And those who do are often only scratching the surface of the intelligence available.

Beyond the obvious cases where active threats are being communicated with the clear use of the brand or organization or individual's name, there exist far more dangerous activities organized and carried out just below the surface—yet still in plain view of those willing to look.

Reputational Deafness

By the end of 2008, America's financial and housing markets were teetering on the brink of collapse. For many, ground zero of the financial crisis was 1 Water Street, New York, NY—the headquarters of American International Group, Inc. (AIG). History would record this period as the beginning of the Great Recession.

The "too big to fail" insurance giant's business model had imploded as a perfect storm burst both the housing and the financial markets' bubbles simultaneously. The previous years' bull market had propelled the company to sell insurance against investment losses for collateralized debt obligations, or CDOs. These CDOs comprised bundles of mortgages, which defaulted when the housing bubble burst. Called to pay out on the CDO insurance they had sold investors, AIG quickly lost over $25 billion. They were in danger of collapse—an event that many feared would cause a cascading effect across the global financial markets, setting off a chain reaction many believed would be unstoppable. To prevent that from happening, the U.S. government issued a $150 billion bailout, in exchange for nearly 80 percent of the company's equity.

It was not the end of the bad news for AIG; in fact, it was really only the beginning of the public relations fall out. In March 2009, it became public that more than $100 million in annual bonuses had been paid out at the end of 2008 to AIG's financial executives—the very executives that the public viewed as responsible for the unstable CDO insurance that led to their downfall. The outcry was intense. It was at that time that I found myself at AIG's headquarters in the center of this storm, brought in to help tackle an incredibly serious and dangerous situation that was brewing.

A search online for reports of the 2009 AIG protests reveals just how vitriolic the anger had become. Protests were launched at AIG offices around the country. Pictures of executives with their children were posted online, along with the addresses of the schools they attended. Multiple death threats were posted freely, with one protester holding a sign declaring that he wanted to "hang [AIG] up with piano wire."

Working together with the communications and corporate security teams, we developed targeted digital listening efforts to better ensure that the human capital of the company—its workers and their families—were being protected. As we began building an aggressive reputation management program to respond to the long-term damage to their brand, we discovered that specific activist groups were organizing in plain sight on Facebook and other websites and blogs. We also realized many of the company's executives' home addresses and deeply personal family details had been exposed. AIG needed to know how this happened and what these activist groups were planning.

As the crisis unfolded, the leaders entrusted with corporate security were increasingly perplexed by what appeared to be sophisticated intelligence gathering efforts. Specifically, the groups were able to zero in directly on the unlisted home addresses of many of their most senior leaders. We identified planned routes for bus tours and protests staged in front of executives' homes, in what was coined the "Lifestyles of the Rich and Infamous" bus tour. As we dug in, our digital listening team soon determined the culprit hiding in plain sight.

Like most Fortune 1000 companies, many of AIG's executives had a history of making political contributions to candidates running for office. Prior to the internet, records of these contributions would be filed away in cavernous federal election files, never to see the light of day. But in the transparent digital era, all these files are now posted to the website opensecrets.org, which includes the full name and personal address—as required by law—of any donor contributing over $1000. Opposition groups had simply identified lists of all AIG executives and began compiling home addresses and spousal information from the open web to support their threatening efforts.

The active listening efforts we deployed at the time enabled the corporate security teams to both detect the security threat (the addresses exposed) and access real-time intelligence on the plans of the activists, who were using Facebook's events tool to coordinate the bus trips. This enabled advance notification to local police departments to be on alert. The information uncovered about individual executives and their families allowed for extra precautions to be taken to ensure their safety. Thankfully, no one was hurt.

This work didn't require cloak-and-dagger level intelligence. It simply required the willingness to listen. It was all being posted in plain view on message boards and comment sections of easily accessible websites.

Market-melting disasters are not the only times we see activist groups organizing openly today. Unions regularly organize on Facebook and Reddit and on other public message boards. Many utilize a variety of networking tools to schedule the date and time of picket lines and other protest efforts. An enterprising crisis team listening to not just their own reputation but to the activities of their detractors would not only be aware of the impending activities, but would also know exactly when, where, and how many protesters to expect.

Proactive Crisis Management

Many high-profile individuals, businesses, and controversial non-profits have at one time or another, perhaps through no fault of their own, landed on the radar of organized opposition groups. These could be labor unions opposed to a business model, environmentalists opposed to the ingredients used in a particular product, political activist groups simply opposed to your very existence, and the list goes on. The genesis of the opposition is irrelevant; recognizing the fact that these groups and individuals exist is key. There is a veritable outrage machine for nearly every sector of our economy that is incentivized to stir the pot as often as possible, driving sensational, click-bait headlines without concern for truth or fairness. Nearly two-thirds of business executives surveyed in 2021 said they believed their companies would face an activist-led crisis situation in the next few years. Unfortunately, what often starts as alarming rumors online can quickly transform into perilous actions manifesting in threats of violence or riots. In some cases, the risk of not listening online extends beyond financial or reputational harm to truly dangerous personal harm.

Those best-prepared have embraced the underlying truth that crisis management starts during the relative "peacetime," long before conflict emerges on the crisis battlefield. During this quiet before the storm, crisis programs need to actively monitor not just their own reputations, but the activities of those most likely to inflict harm upon them.

There are multiple inexpensive (and many free) tools available to crisis managers today, enabling easy and real-time capabilities to sift through the noise to find the actionable intelligence needed to stay one step ahead in a crisis. The easiest and most often overlooked is a simple Google News Alert. Setting these alerts up for organizational names, brands, products, and key leaders is a bare minimum requirement. Seeking advanced tools that leverage artificial intelligence to sort through the noise has become, for most, table stakes. Consider the previous stories involving tens of thousands, if not millions of posts. Humans alone cannot possibly sift through the data in real time to determine the most influential voices leading the charge.

Trying to deploy these tools for the first time in the middle of a crisis is less than ideal. From a purely practical standpoint, the software licensing, stakeholder mapping, and account setup process can take days if not weeks to accomplish, depending on the size and complexity of the organization.

No one can afford to fly blind and deaf for that long in a crisis.

Those responsible for monitoring the online discourse need to be trained to identify not just the obvious angry customer post, but the less obvious threats as well. This is where many organizations fail to truly leverage the fire-fighting capability of social listening, by leaving their monitoring programs to junior marketing teams to manage. Rather than counting on marketing social media teams to have a clear understanding of the crisis landscape, reporting protocols for elevating threats beyond the walls of the customer service or marketing teams need to be established early on. Not every critical social media post is a crisis. Part of an effective program is understanding which voices matter—which commentators can actually shape public opinion. Understanding how to sift through the noise, through the millions of posts that happen every moment, to identify the match that could ignite your crisis fire takes time and investment.

Further, if your organization does have a listening program, you need to ensure you have established clear procedures to notify members of the crisis team should damaging information be discovered. Listening without training your team what to do when they hear something critical is a lost opportunity.

When done right, listening programs not only limit the impact of a crisis, they can, if deployed effectively, cut them off before they metastasize into a corporation-killing cancer. In his book *Customer CEO*, author Chuck Wall recounts the story of how L.L. Bean embraced and invested in active listening programs and cross-team collaboration. The company's social and digital media monitoring team had noticed that a popular fitted sheet was getting an outsized number of negative online reviews. It was not a crisis per se, but it was a clear anomaly that the monitoring team had been trained to look for and empowered to report.

As the report made its way to the quality control team, the company decided to remove the sheets from the website until it was able to identify what was causing the uptick in complaints online. As it turned out, a vendor had made a manufacturing mistake that was causing the fabric to fail.

L.L. Bean's chief marketing officer Steve Fuller said of the incident, "Before, it would have taken us months and months to figure out if something was wrong with the product through returns, if we ever would have known at all." The ability to connect active listening with broader business functions was key to the brand's success. If they were not listening, they never would have been able to hear the concerns, and more importantly, save time and money while avoiding the potential for reputation damage from unhappy customer comments continuing to populate online.

CHAPTER 4
KEEP YOUR FRIENDS CLOSE

*"At every crisis in one's life, it is absolute
salvation to have some sympathetic
friend to whom you can think aloud
without restraint or misgiving."*

–Woodrow Wilson

In 2012, Johnson & Johnson rolled out a safer dispenser cap for their product, Infants' Tylenol. I had the opportunity to work with J&J during this time, just as they started to realize that parents were experiencing a recurring problem with the new cap. One of the unintended consequences of the new safety packaging was leading some parents to apply too much pressure on the dispenser cap, inadvertently breaking the dispenser. Johnson & Johnson discovered that while there were absolutely no safety concerns with the actual medicine, even the hint of a recall managed incorrectly could discourage parents from shopping for the brand.

J&J has a long history embracing transparency and its corporate beliefs are founded on a long-held sense of putting the customer first. Their response efforts to the 1980s Tylenol recall are still mandatory reading in nearly every business school in America, and they will be analyzed in a subsequent chapter in this book.

While the brand's commitment to putting its customers first had not changed in the years since the sensational Tylenol recall, nearly everything else about their crisis planning protocols had. Johnson & Johnson knew instinctively that misinformation would flow faster than truth and that they could not carry the day against a sea of potential negativity without a new playbook to support their efforts.

Working with the company's digital team, we identified high-profile mom bloggers and tweeters with whom we could proactively engage with, to ensure they were aware of the extraordinary steps the company was taking to remove a product that worked perfectly fine but that had an unfortunate packaging defect. These moms were not paid shills; these were trusted parent voices with no connection to Tylenol, who we had identified through a targeted social listening effort as being influential voices capable of shaping public opinion. For example, actress and influencer Alyssa Milano had been identified as a trusted source for many moms at the time. The crisis team engaged her and many other mom-influencers early with videos and information to educate their followers about the product. Consequently, the actress (and many others) became one of many voices helping to calm parents' concerns.

Johnson & Johnson also identified the top hospital and pediatric Twitter handles and Facebook pages across the country and opened a dialogue with the moderators to ensure those on the frontlines of the healthcare information wars had the accurate information necessary to educate parents. We knew instinctively that in a crisis moment, especially one that involves children, parents would turn to their local doctors and hospitals for trusted information.

When the time came to ultimately withdraw the product to fix the packaging, J&J developed a series of informational videos with nurses and moms in both Spanish and English, explaining the appropriate way to use the dispenser. The videos provided the identified groups of digital influencers with easy-to-share content that assuaged concerns about the safety of the actual pain reliever, making it clear the issue was simply a packaging flaw unrelated to the efficacy of the actual product.

Media outlets and many hospitals began retweeting the information as a public information service, and J&J was once again credited with its efforts to put families first. The company won the day and avoided becoming the target of criticism because they took the time to know the trusted voices in their space before they needed them. And then, equally important, they armed those influential voices with the tools needed to take the correct messaging to the public.

Ask yourself the following questions: If you needed a hundred people to take up arms and join you in becoming digital apostles during a crisis right now, do you know who those credible third-party individuals are? How about fifty? Ten? Do you have strong relationships with passionate brand advocates who will stand ground next to you during even the most intense fights? Have you used your crisis peacetime wisely to cultivate these ambassadors, to give them a sense of shared commitment to your success so that when your crisis moment comes, they are not only ready to answer the call to defend the walls, but feel a sense of obligation to do so?

The age-old admonition to know your friends before you need them has never been more relevant than in today's crisis world. Take the time now to identify your most passionate supporters online. Tie them tightly to your brand or cause and give them a reason to invest in your success. Build special communities that provide extra access to insider information, special deals, or one-on-one chats to deepen the ties that bind you to your most loyal supporters. Let these warriors-in-waiting know that you value them before you need them. And when the time comes, arm them for battle with easily sharable content—videos, blog posts, infographics, memes, photos, and tweets—necessary to turn back the tide.

And, while your apostles are spreading the good news, ensure you understand how to sort through the firestorm of negativity to identify, engage, and hopefully neutralize the real antagonists fanning the flames.

CHAPTER 5

KEEP YOUR ENEMIES CLOSER

"If you want peace, you don't talk to your friends. You talk to your enemies."

—Desmond Tutu

When a crisis hits, it can seem at times as if every single person on the planet with an internet connection or smartphone is an expert on your organization. No doubt the voices will clamor that any response or action you take could have been more thoughtfully executed.

The fire hose of criticism that will be unleashed during a crisis across television news, blogs, X (Twitter), comment boards, and other digital mediums will begin to feel like the proverbial death by a thousand cuts. In an intense crisis, the ability to decipher which critics count the most will, in many cases, determine the success or failure of your engagement efforts. Your instincts will guide you to want to reply to every false rumor or insulting comment that comes your way. It is a natural reaction. And while it may in fact feel good, it is simply not sustainable when you find yourself facing hundreds, if not tens of thousands of vitriolic commentators.

It is in these moments of incoming fire when it will be critical to have the insights necessary to identify the voices that are capable of inflicting the *most* reputational harm, as well as those voices capable of calming the seas. In Chapter 3, we discussed the importance of having listening tools in place ahead of your crisis and Chapter 4 outlined the value of having brand apostles at the ready to support your cause. Operationalizing these tools effectively is the next step.

Not every tweeter is equal. Not every blogger or Tik-Toker deserves a thoughtful response. With every minute counting, you need to know who is organizing and influencing the mob—not just who has picked up a pitchfork to join the charge.

Having managed literally hundreds of crises in my career, I still find myself surprised at who many of the most influential opposition voices turn out to be. Many are the obvious culprits, but rarely are they all who you would expect, as IKEA found out.

A Furniture Fiasco

The popular family-friendly bargain furniture retailer found itself in unfamiliar territory, facing intense scrutiny for its decision to airbrush images of women out of its seasonal catalog in Saudi Arabia. Swedish publication *Metro* broke the story, showing side-by-side comparisons of IKEA's Swedish catalog vs. the Saudi catalog. While localizing marketing materials to respect cultural norms has been a long-standing practice in the advertising world, in today's digital connected marketplace, the stark contrast of the imagery went viral. Digital was the accelerant to this crisis fire. Once the spark was lit, it was merely a matter of hours before IKEA was facing an onslaught of angry customers and activist groups from around the globe.

On any given day prior to this incident, IKEA would experience about 20,000 mentions on social media. Once *Metro*'s story caught wind, however, that number tripled, and the commentary was overwhelmingly negative. It was an unprecedented storm of criticism for the brand, and there was no way to engage in hand-to-hand combat with every angry voice.

IKEA had already established a strong social media presence and had a committed group of brand apostles ready to charge the hill in the event their favorite purveyor of Swedish meatballs and dorm room furniture needed a hand. While helpful to their marketing efforts in good times, this was a totally different conversation. Many of IKEA's most loyal fans and brand ambassadors were left unengaged during the crisis—leaving a critical arrow unused in IKEA's crisis quiver.

IKEA was not being attacked for a product, but for violating a cultural norm. The global conversation was being driven by an entirely new group of digital influencers with whom the brand had previously never engaged with.

Where college-bound students, moms, and DIYers once shaped the brand's conversation, IKEA now found itself parrying jibes from people like Oxford professor Richard Dawkins; Miguel Otero, editor of the Venezuelan publication *El Nacional*; and actors Alister Cameron and Pam Grier—each of whom had nearly half a million followers on Twitter. And while the seventies cult favorite Foxy Brown may not have been on their radar prior to the crisis, IKEA had already invested in the muscle memory necessary to understand how to read online conversations and decipher who the most influential voices were at any given time. This ability to rapidly identify who was driving the social conversation and develop targeted response efforts played a critical role in stopping the flood of criticism before the brand was overwhelmed and a highly critical narrative about the company took hold indelibly.

Thankfully in today's modern marketing and communications world, there are multiple free and for-purchase tools available to help identify which voices matter and which don't. It is mission critical to have these resources available *before* your crisis occurs. Learning to build profiles and train teams how to appropriately weigh the relevance of the conversations occurring in the most fragmented media landscape we have ever seen—while the building is on fire—is not a recipe for success.

The Chinese use two brush strokes to write the word crisis. The first brush stroke spells danger. And there is indeed great risk in engaging opposition forces in a crisis. However, the second brush stroke spells opportunity and, as we will see in later chapters, there can be immense opportunity to co-opt the forces initially aligned against you in a crisis if you play your cards right.

Determining which opposition voices can inflict the greatest harm to your reputation is an important first step. But it is simply a defensive step. You cannot win a crisis battle on defensive tactics alone.

CHAPTER 6

KEEP THE PRESS (AND THE ROBOTS) CLOSEST

*"In America, the president reigns
for four years, and journalism
governs forever and ever."*

–Oscar Wilde.

The state of journalism is changing dramatically, with a constant revolving door of publications announcing layoffs throughout the initial years of the 2020s. According to a 2021 survey by Muck Rack, the average reporter now covers three different media beats and has more work than ever before. One journalist friend at a major industry publication shared with me that she was filing one to two stories per day. The journalists who are left in the field find that their influence is increasing at the same rate that their time and availability for pitches is decreasing.

Another well-known reporter shared with me that her most precious commodity was time. "I pick and choose which events I attend based on my ability to maximize time. We have so little today," she shared in one off-the-record gathering. It has never been harder—or more vital—to know these key gatekeepers to public opinion. Just as it is important to have relationships with potential brand advocates, social influencers, and passionate dyed-in-the-wool fans, knowing the key reporters in your field could be your saving grace in a moment of crisis.

This may seem beyond obvious, but after more than twenty years in the media relations trenches working both inside some of the largest public companies and outside for some of the largest global PR agencies, I have discovered an alarming decline in relationship management between the professionals charged with crafting a story and those in the media paid to actually tell it. Far too often, the key relationships are left to be managed by outside agencies. The fundamental shortsightedness of this approach becomes clear when viewed through a crisis lens. Consider the campaign in 2020 by the advocate group Fossil Free Media to force the largest PR agencies in the world to "fire" their fossil fuel clients. PR agencies should be viewed as an extension of your in-house capabilities, not a replacement for them. When a crisis hits, you will want to have already built a well of trust with your key media to draw upon when many others will have turned their backs on you.

When working to build these relations, what must be recognized is that many reporters today simply do not respond (or even read) emails. However, nearly eight out of ten journalists report that they regularly check social media for breaking news updates. Seventy percent use it to see what rival news outlets are covering, six out of ten use social media to develop coverage ideas, and more than half use X (Twitter) to identify sources to interview for their stories. Seventy-six percent of journalists told Muck Rack that X is their most valuable platform, and 37 percent said they plan to use X *more* in the future. Take the time now to follow the key reporters who cover your industry or your set of particular issues on social media. Watch what these reporters post to their channels to understand what they are trying to cover to position your organization as a helpful resource before you need to engage them in a future crisis response.

ABC News Anchor Chris O'Connell shared his experience with social media while covering a major automotive recall, saying: "I routinely track down potential interviewees by sending out a Tweet. Most recently, we came across a number of Toyota car owners who fell under the recent recalls."

You might also consider joining a site like HelpaReporterOut.com (HARO plans to rebrand as Connectively in the next year), which can put you in touch with many smaller media outlet reporters to help establish you as an expert resource. It may seem elementary, but it is absolutely critical to have the mobile numbers of the top reporters who cover your industry. Build a mutually respectful relationship so that you can have a green light to text them whenever news breaks. Most reporters I work with prefer text over any other form of engagement. They have self-selected who they give their cell phone number to, and they enforce rigid rules on who can text them. Being on their "whitelist" will be critical to your efforts of breaking through and reaching those with the most immediate ability—and credibility—to cover your crisis.

Long gone are the days when reporters looked like Perry White, the fictional editor-in-chief of *The Daily Planet* in DC Comics. Perry White has been replaced by X, HARO, Reddit and other outlets that have become the dominant assignment editors and source locators for journalists today. We can lament the loss of the gumshoe reporter, but we ignore the realities of new media reporting at our peril.

When your crisis does finally come, remember that many journalists still move in packs, relying on each other for tips and leads. Find the leader of the pack and bring them into the fold during your crisis. Give them access to you and your people. Displaying an honest attempt at transparency and a willingness to try to do the right thing can go a long way toward shaping coverage in your favor.

You cannot engage with every reporter that may cover your crisis. Find the lead wolves and turn them to your side as best you can. The packs will usually follow.

Rise of the Robots

Beyond working with influential journalists in our new media environment, one cautionary tale illustrates a new challenge that crisis managers need to prepare for: the rise of machine-driven reporting.

As early as 2014, the Associated Press (AP), with no fanfare at all, rolled out a new "automated reporting" feature designed to expand their ability to cover far more financial reporting events each year than their small cadre of financial reporters could manage. While most are familiar with the Fortune 500 companies that drive much of the overall movement of the New York Stock Exchange (NYSE) and NASDAQ markets, there are thousands upon thousands of additional publicly traded companies that few have ever heard of.

These companies trade across the same public exchanges and are required to file the same quarterly statements as Apple or Google. The main difference is that most have never had the pleasure of being covered by a major wire reporter or outlet. All this began to change in late 2014 and took a major turn in 2015 as the AP rolled out automated reporting for the earnings reports of thousands of companies.

At the time, I was leading communications for one of the first companies to ever be caught up in the snare of this new wave of reporting. The experience gave me a searingly up-close glimpse into the challenges smaller market cap companies are facing in the brave new world of robotic journalism. In this world, relationships did not matter, as reporting relied entirely on algorithms to establish headlines, write leading paragraphs, and create the overall tone and content of the entire article. My company had just recently completed its initial public offering (IPO) and was leading in a fast-paced, fast-growth sector of the technology market. The company had just posted fantastic earnings—far out-pacing Wall Street's expectations.

The few analysts that covered the company were over the moon with the report and we expected to see major positive news in the few trade publications that covered our sector. What we did *not* expect to see blaring across our screens was a headline declaring we had produced a significant loss for the quarter. The headline was quickly picked up by Yahoo! News and reposted by CNBC due to a content-sharing partnership the AP had established with both outlets.

Rather than enjoying a celebratory moment in the sun after a strong quarter, we found ourselves on the defensive, trying to track down the AP reporter who had completely misread the meaning of our earnings report. Growth was what analysts were monitoring and the company had crushed expectations. The minutes ticked by until we frantically reached the AP reporter covering technology. We learned that neither he, nor any other reporter on the tech team, had anything to do with the story. Quietly, he grumbled that the erroneous article had been computer generated without review and that he had no power to change the story.

After more than an hour of navigating through the byways of the Associated Press, we managed to track down the editor responsible for the new automated reporting feature. After making the case that while the facts were correct in the story, the entire premise missed the point, the AP assigned a copy editor to manually go into the story and update the content. The new headline touted our topping of quarterly estimates and the new lead-in section now accurately reflected the news. But at this point, the damage was done. The content-sharing partnership with Yahoo! Finance and CNBC did not extend to updates, just original reporting, so even after correcting the official AP record, the misrepresentation lingered in public view.

By 2021, artificial intelligence-driven news reporting had expanded significantly. Media outlets were using the capabilities of machine learning to develop the most click-worthy headlines and some outlets, such as the *Miami Herald*, assigned entire news beats to robots. As Jeremy Gilbert, director of strategic initiatives for *The Washington Post* said at the time: "I think there are a lot of different, pretty interesting things we can do with A.I., and it runs the gamut from tools that assist humans with their reporting to algorithms that actually tell stories directly from data." Two years later in 2023, *The Guardian* newspaper had identified more than fifty news websites with content that was entirely AI generated. Also, in 2023, NewsCorp began deploying AI to manage coverage of thousands of local stories in Australia. Everywhere you looked, it appeared the robots were on the march. The rising risk from these robo-generated stories became a headline-blaring crisis in and of itself for one media company as CNET's AI-generated stories were found to have so many errors the media outlet pulled the plug, but not before facing headlines like: "Plagued with errors: A news outlet's decision to write stories with AI backfires" which CNN was only too happy to file, with human hands.

The key takeaway here is that in today's digitally driven world, many of the norms have changed. More than a decade ago, after my first encounter with the AP's AI, we added an entire new layer to our earnings media prep that now included briefing the automated reporting team in advance of filing to ensure a human reviewed the auto-generated report for the correct tone and positioning. The robots are not totally in control just yet, but it is still better to have them on your side.

CHAPTER 7
AVOID RISK FROM WITHIN

"Think about how stupid the average person is, and then realize that half of 'em are stupider than that."

-George Carlin

The world of new media emerged during my time serving on Secretary of Defense Donald H. Rumsfeld's communications team at the Pentagon in the early 2000s. Suddenly, the military's ability to control the dissemination of information from the front lines of the Iraq War—and from all four corners of the world where the US military was actively engaged in the global war on terror—was jeopardized.

Press reports on combat operations, including footage from videos posted by our troops in the field, were being filed before many in the Pentagon had even seen the official after-action report. During this time, a US service member serving abroad was accused of a serious violation of the uniform code of military justice—the laws that govern the lives of every service member, regardless of the country in which they are serving. That this memory has stayed so strongly with me has little to do with the fact that somewhere on the planet one of the two-million-plus men and women serving our country made a mistake—even a terrible mistake. The law of averages for human screwups would almost demand it. Why this particular incident remains so memorable to me is because of the reaction one senior Pentagon leader had at the time the news broke.

"Somewhere, in one of the 100+ countries our young folks are serving in, I can guarantee you someone is doing something unbelievably stupid every day," said the official. "The difference is, now those actions are being filmed and posted and shared online for all to see."

Young men and women (and old ones, too) in extremely tense situations are going to make mistakes. Unfortunately, with the accelerant of social media, those mistakes will be amplified online, bringing to light a new risk for employers. No matter how big or small an organization is, the public today will hold the *employer* responsible for the transgressions of its employees.

The Personal Is Organizational

To help illustrate the perils of failing to safeguard against employee-inflicted reputational damage, one can look back in time to the most recent large-scale Israeli and Palestinian military conflict in Gaza prior to the horrific events of 2023. As NBC News reported at the time with its headline "The

New Propaganda: Armies Take War to Twitter in Gaza Conflict," both the Israeli military and Hamas had established a new beachhead in the 2010s on Twitter to fight the information war. The new front was less about winning tactical ground battles and more about "trying to win the hearts and minds of watchers around the globe." Quoting from NBC News coverage of the Twitter battle: "Now, the Israeli Defense Forces and the Hamas military Al Qassam Brigades are taking to Twitter, Facebook, YouTube and Flickr, instantly sharing photos, videos and granular news bites in English, so that they can reach the broadest possible audience." We would see this same playbook play out from Israel and Gaza once again with a steady stream of heartbreaking images of death and destruction a decade later.

As the conflict on the ground and across social channels heated up in 2012, the Israeli Defense Force's (IDF) point person for social media engagement, a twenty-six-year-old Israeli Lieutenant named Sacha Dratwa, began to garner a lot of personal media attention for his cutting-edge use of the Twitter platform as a strategy in war. *Business Insider* named the military tweeter one of the fifty most influential people at the forefront of "political innovation" at the time. In its write up of Lt. Dratwa, the media outlet claimed that his work for the IDF's social media presence for the past two years had "turned it into the most globally visible arm of the Israeli military."

The IDF decided to brand this soldier as the "face" of their global social media effort. He was offered up for media interviews and speeches, and highlighted as the future of modern wartime communications. There was only one problem. For all Dratwa's prowess at using social media in the workplace, he was utterly unprepared for how to manage his own personal social reputation.

Half a world away, while Dratwa was fighting the propaganda war in Israel, then President Barack Obama was fighting for his political life during the November 2012 re-election. Nasty issues of race had entered the campaign in the final months. Around this time, our intrepid Israeli social media expert posted an image of himself at the Dead Sea with mud on his face to his personal Facebook page. This type of photo would not usually cause much notice or alarm. But much to the dismay of his military commanders, Dratwa captioned the photo "Obama style."

The social media darling's house came crashing down with the reference to President Obama while in clear "black face," a poorly timed insult to the leader of one of Israel's most staunch allies. Headlines blared: "Military head of social media slammed for black face." The Israeli government was forced to issue an apology to the United States. Dratwa's initial public response in the early hours of the brewing crisis serves to further highlight his lack of training, which should be necessary for all employees, let alone someone on the media front lines.

"There have been attempts to make use of private photos from my Facebook profile in order to publicly misrepresent my opinions," Dratwa told the media. "Due to the amount of public attention I've garnered in recent days, I have decided to restrict access to my page in order to protect my privacy and prevent further cynical use of the information therein. I am, and have always been, completely candid about my beliefs and have nothing to hide—as reflected by my Facebook profile which, until recently, was open to everyone." For all his young promise, the very fact that he believed information posted to his personal social media accounts—information that was open for the world to see—was somehow "private" and off limits showed his naivety and misunderstanding of the nature of the new media world. Sadly, it led to his undoing and to the embarrassment of his organizational leadership.

Just because someone is a social media starlet with thousands of followers and an always-ready Instagrammable pose, does not mean they have a clue about reputation management. Let that sink in for a moment when you then realize 99 percent of your colleagues have only a fraction of Lieutenant Sacha Dratwa's social media savvy.

Everyone Is a Social Media Novice

It is not just young members of the military making these mistakes. Seasoned executives at the biggest technology and media companies are still learning how to avoid reputational pitfalls in the social sphere. In June 2021, Google was forced to remove a senior executive on its diversity team over a fourteen-year-old blog post that surfaced claiming that Jews had an "insatiable appetite for war."

In 2017, following the mass shooting in Las Vegas at a country music festival that left more than fifty people dead and hundreds more injured, a senior legal executive at CBS posted the following to her Facebook page: "If they wouldn't do anything when children were murdered, I have no hope that Repubs will ever do the right thing. I'm actually not even sympathetic because country music fans often are Republican gun toters."

Center-right media outlets jumped on this comment as representative of what many conservatives believe to be left-leaning media bias. In short order, thousands had signed a petition urging the New York Bar Association to investigate. CBS, now facing a serious media backlash of its own, quickly decided to fire the executive.

The lessons from these instances are twofold. First, even those who appear to be social media savvy, or legally trained, or deeply embedded in the digital ecosystem, can and will make poor decisions on social media for all the world to see. In today's 1440 news cycle, there is no "private" social media. The second lesson is that responsibility for these missteps will be shared in the eyes of the public. Regardless of the level of direct knowledge of an employee's error (or lack thereof), there is no doubt that the organization and its leaders will be called to answer for it.

Organizations need to ensure they have invested in the right training measures to protect both their employees' and their organization's reputations. The Israeli military public affairs commanders should never have allowed an individual to have such a high-profile presence without doing some basic background monitoring and providing training for Dratwa. Google executives should have known about the fourteen-year-old blog post and had a plan ready to address it, if and when the issue arose. One old statement does not need to cause a crisis or lead to a loss of employment if the team understood the circumstances and gotten ahead of it internally and publicly. On a very tactical level, no employee should be hired today without a thorough vetting of their past social media activity. Every employee should understand that in today's always-on and always-connected social world, the lines between personal and professional commentary have not just blurred; they have disappeared entirely.

Given this reality, it has become all the more urgent for organizations to develop effective training programs designed to educate employees on effective social media usage. Just as we train for sexual harassment or antidiscrimination policies, we must also educate staff—no matter their age or assumed social media proficiency—to recognize that in the age of social media, there is no privacy. Every action can reflect on both the individual and the employer.

The first and most obvious step in developing effective training is to create a social media usage policy for your organization. You cannot stop humans from posting or being social; it is how we communicate today. Having a policy that begins with "do not use social media" will be about as useful as a screen door on a submarine. Developing a comprehensive policy that trains and equips your workforce for how to build a professional career and leverage the incredible tools of social media for personal and professional growth will serve to unleash the creative power of your workforce—which could, in times of crisis, be an incredibly useful resource. In Chapter 25, how to deploy internal employees as advocates in a crisis will be covered. But before getting to how to leverage the positive, you must first ensure every employee, in the words of Warren Buffett, "knows what they are doing" when it comes to social media engagement.

Everyone in your organization will benefit from clear "how to" rules and training for social media that encourages them to be authentic while avoiding unnecessary risks.

CHAPTER 8

CORPORATE RESPONSIBILITY IN THE AGE OF ACTIVISM

"If you are neutral in situations of injustice, you have chosen the side of the oppressor."

–Desmond Tutu

I n 2018, another example of employee misconduct revealed the extent to which organizations are called to account for not just their employees' behaviors, but also their integrity in upholding company values.

Starbucks prides itself on being the neighborhood coffee shop, a "third place" (besides home and work) where you are free to gather safely as a vital part of the fabric of a community. On April 12, 2018, two young black men walked into a Philadelphia Starbucks for a meeting—an act so innocuous you can image it happening daily in any one of the more than 8,000 Starbucks locations nationwide. But, unfortunately, in the City of Brotherly Love, a spark was about to be ignited that would either shake the company to its foundation, or propel it forward to positive change.

Upon seeing two black men in the store who had not ordered drinks, the Philadelphia Starbucks manager decided to call the police and have the men removed. When the police arrived, rather than deescalate the situation, they arrested the men while every cell phone camera within reach recorded and broadcast the scene. The news went viral almost immediately.

Fully five years after the first appearance of #blacklivesmatter as a trending topic on Twitter and three years after the death of Michael Brown in Ferguson, MO, the American public was engaged in the most substantive conversation about race relations our nation had witnessed in nearly half a century. It would still be another two years before the horrifying death of George Floyd at the hands of Minneapolis police officers would truly galvanize the nation for change. However, by 2018 it was clear that our decades-long dialogue on race relations was reaching a turning point. The story of how Starbucks stumbled, and then regained its footing in the age of political activism offers telling insights for those with reputations worth preserving.

As the media onslaught engulfing Starbucks launched protests and boycotts nationwide, the urge to reactively engage was likely overpowering. Instinctively, Starbucks had to know it was moving out of their control.

"We had to move quickly, yes, but resist responding to questions until I knew in my heart I was ready to answer them.... My larger responsibility was to review every aspect of what happened, then make an assessment, and then do everything I could to ensure it didn't happen again," said Starbucks CEO Kevin Johnson after the dust settled. Johnson was right, of course; the instinct to engage immediately can be overpowering, and if done poorly, it can come back to haunt you.

During those initial hours, the Starbucks team was clearly trying to ascertain as much information as possible before responding. They recognized the risk of saying too much too soon. But they made the mistake of falling into binary thinking; to say something or not to say something is not an all-or-nothing deliberation.

In the first forty-eight hours after the incident, Starbucks avoided saying too much. The problem was, they said nothing at all. That silence created a vacuum that angry social media posts and organized protesters were more than ready to fill, positioning Starbucks as another example of an out-of-touch company that was part of the race relations problem in America. Two days after the video went viral, Philadelphia Mayor Jim Kenney released a statement saying the incident "appears to exemplify what racial discrimination looks like in 2018."

Looking back on the crisis, Johnson said there was "no playbook for how you handle a crisis like this." In this, he could not have been more wrong. Starbucks's initial misread of the situation led to an unnecessarily agonizing delay of action that nearly buried the company reputationally. What is so telling about Johnson's reaction is that even with all the company's previously well-documented crisis stumbles,

Starbucks was still groping in the dark during the initial hours of what was turning into a national nightmare for the company.

In short order, Starbucks had become the poster child for the deteriorating state of racial discrimination in America. As the furor mounted, Starbucks finally released a statement via Twitter that served to only compound the perception of being out of touch. They issued a faceless, emotionless corporate statement that lacked any human recognition of the gravity of the situation or the painful history the incident represented for so many people of color in America.

The first quarter of the crisis game clock had ticked down and, by all accounts, the company had fumbled the ball. This story could easily have continued down the same path that others who lawyered-up and hunkered-down have experienced. In so many instances where engagement is delayed and messaging is stymied because of risk, the crisis can metastasize, leaving a lasting and powerfully negative overhang on a reputation.

While Starbucks has been rightly criticized for the delayed reaction during the initial days of their crisis, what happened next changed the game entirely.

Pivoting Successfully

The world was now watching and listening to see what Starbucks did next. This is yet another important lesson that most fail to recognize. There are times in a crisis when it is not just about extinguishing the fire. There will be moments when a window is opened, ever so slightly, to pivot the entire discussion and build positive momentum from the pain. Starbucks grabbed that moment. On April 17, five days after the video exploded on social media, the company announced it would be closing all stores for a full day of racial bias training.

In a heartfelt interview with CBS the next day, then-Chairman Howard Schultz offered a genuine apology, delivering a message of welcome to everyone regardless of race or any other factor, and promising that the company would take immediate action to change. Reflecting on what he was thinking during the first twenty-four hours of the crisis, Schultz shared: "In my heart, I believed that the incident had the potential to be a positive galvanizing moment. An opportunity for growth. How we responded would reinforce our core values, and make us better."

In the darkest moment, Starbucks realized there was an opportunity to take this crisis spark and transform it into a beacon for positive change. The company had built an ethos around their cultural values, and therefore, the expectation from the public and from their own employees was that they would live up to those values. They immediately changed tactic and leaned into that expectation. Johnson, the CEO, followed up the initial cold corporate statement with a personal post that showed for the first time that Starbucks employees were hurting too. "The video shot by customers is very hard to watch and the actions in it are not representative of our Starbucks Mission and Values," he wrote. He went on to say: "Creating an environment that is both safe and welcoming for everyone is paramount for every store. Regretfully, our practices and training led to a bad outcome. The basis for the call to the Philadelphia police department was wrong." In taking responsibility for the wrong decision—the police never should have been called—Johnson echoed Schultz's words and acknowledged the error was on their side.

Starbucks's successful pivot illustrates a core truth that all leaders need to embrace today: When your organization (or you personally) transgresses—especially in a way that fails to honor a person's dignity and humanity, and that fails to uphold stated values—the first and only appropriate response is an apology. Recognize the damage that was done to others. Own your mistake entirely. Be fully present and engaged. By apologizing, Johnson made it clear this was not going to be brushed under the carpet. He went on a national media tour and flew to Philadelphia. Starbucks moved out from behind a faceless corporate approach and put the CEO front and center. They owned the mistake and promised action.

The Starbucks case is a telling example of both initial failure and eventual success for those with reputations worth defending. While Starbucks got a good deal right, their early missteps were nearly fatal. Johnson's refrain that there was "no playbook" foreshadowed the stumble the company faced out of the gate. Ironically giving in to the all-too-human tendency to hide and armor up, the company had initially adopted an inhuman approach lacking any empathy or recognition. The crisis raged untended for forty-eight hours, an eternity in today's rapid news cycle. Eventually, Starbucks recovered and got to work rectifying their mistakes. But there is nothing in Johnson's eventual open letter that could not have been posted within the initial hours of the incident. The fine line between saying too much and not saying enough is incredibly perilous. And when the offensive actions result in personal harm against anyone, there is simply no time to delay.

Not every company can close for an entire day. Not every organization will face a headline-glaring racial bias case. But every company should have the playbook at hand and be ready to step into the crisis arena with focus, empathy, and a commitment to right whatever wrong has occurred.

I would like to leave a closing thought on changing employee expectations today as it relates to corporate engagement in political or public policy issues. Americans are more politically polarized than they have been in half a century. Social norms around gender, race, sexual orientation, immigration, foreign policy, and a host of additional issues bubble up almost daily. The pull to lean in and lend a voice of support for a particular issue that impacts employees or customers will present itself again and again in the coming years. Debates about whether to recognize certain social, ethnic, or gender community moments in time, or support headline making moments like Ukraine in 2022 or Israel in 2024 will come and go. In the moment there may be significant pressure internally and externally to "take a stand."

Starbucks was particularly exposed by the incident in Philadelphia because the company had made corporate social responsibility a core pillar of its business. It invited the masses to judge the company by the positions they took, from fair trade coffee to recycled paper goods and more. They set the bar (high as it turns out) by which their actions to "take a stand" would be viewed and when they failed to meet the standard they were taken to the woodshed.

Not every company has to take a political stand. Not every moment requires or even deserves commentary from company leadership. In fact, the very concept of businesses taking a position is politically divisive itself. A 2023 Gallup poll found Americans evenly split about whether businesses should "take a public stance on political and social issues." According to Gallup, 48 percent of Americans believe companies should take a stand and 52 percent believe they should simply stay out of the fray. The numbers bend depending on age groups with nearly six in ten adults under thirty believing companies have a responsibility to engage and nearly the exact same percentages (six in ten) of those over forty-one saying companies shouldn't engage.

All of this is to say, if your organization has not staked its reputation on taking political positions, the country is split on whether they even want to hear from you. Don't be pressured by the movement of the moment into "taking action" if it is not core to the DNA of the business or truly important to those working on your team. Once you gave set the precedent of engagement, the genie is hard to get back in the bottle.

One business I was associated with navigated the particularly thorny issue of employee expectations with a two-pronged approach that empowered its workforce to do the good they felt most drawn to. The company policy was clear: There would be no statements from the business about anything political or policy related. At the same time, the company offered two days a year of paid leave to volunteer for causes important to individuals and they offered to match employee donations to non-profits up to two hundred dollars.

Finally, remember that the actions of any leadership team directly reflect on the entire business, even if they are personal. While your organization may avoid politically sensitive issues, your personal decision to write a check to a political candidate or support publicly a sensitive issue is fair game for your employees and the public to weigh in judgment. Just as we learned from the "personal" social media posts that flared into crisis moments in the previous chapter, in today's connected information world, there are no barriers between personal or political or business matters.

CHAPTER 9

USE YOUR PEACETIME WISELY

"In times of peace, prepare for war."

–Niccolò Machiavelli

The clarity that comes from facing down a crisis situation is hard to describe. As the crisis rages, you will see clearly all the things you wish you had done to better prepare. The litany of items you will wish you had invested in could range from the obscenely obvious ("I can't believe we didn't think of that") to the far more nuanced and specific needs that had likely never crossed your mind before reading this book.

Time and again in a crisis, organizations discover that they have not effectively bulletproofed their reputations to withstand an attack. This lack of planning usually stems from a financial analysis that finds the cost of good planning outweighs the risk of a crisis occurring. This would be like not investing in flood insurance when you live near a river, just because the river does not happen to flood *that* often. As you can imagine, this shortsighted approach sets an organization up for far greater financial harm when their crisis card is called. The age-old saying that an ounce of prevention is worth a pound of cure has never been more relevant.

Returning to Johnson & Johnson, we see another example of the value found in proactively minding the reputational shop.

In 2012—six years after Twitter was created—Johnson & Johnson had still not activated a Tylenol-branded Twitter account, even despite the recent recall of Infants Tylenol. At the time, Twitter wasn't seen as a necessary platform for proactive marketing or public relations, so no one had taken the time to even look into reserving the account. Remember, this was still a year before the Boston Marathon bombing made Twitter the ultimate crisis response platform.

As various crises began emerging in social media, J&J's digital reputation management team decided to fix this oversight and reserve the username @Tylenol to engage in tough conversations should the brand face a future crisis on social media. But when they investigated, J&J discovered that an individual had already squatted on the @Tylenol account, marketing it as "the home of the hangover cure" and plastering the feed with J&J branded imagery.

J&J quickly remedied the situation, requesting Twitter re-assign their copyright-protected moniker back to the company—a request Twitter has established policies for reviewing and approving. Johnson & Johnson used its peacetime wisely to identify and claim the channels it would need when—not if—its next crisis occurred, and they took proactive steps to defend against the possibility of future brand-jacking attempts. Today, thousands of parents, doctors, hospitals, and journalists follow @Tylenol for important updates from the brand.

British Petroleum's handling of the Deepwater Horizon oil disaster serves as a compelling counterexample to Johnson & Johnson and shows why advance planning is so critical to the chances of crisis survival.

Steering Through Stormy Waters

On April 20, 2010, the largest environmental disaster of the new millennium was bubbling just below the surface of the Gulf of Mexico. That day, the Deepwater Horizon oil rig exploded and burned off the coast of Louisiana, killing eleven crewmembers and releasing approximately 134 million gallons of oil into the ocean. The events that led up to the now infamous oil spill have become the fodder of movie lore, thanks to the 2016 Hollywood blockbuster of the same name. And while the massive environmental impact, courtroom legal drama, and the billions of dollars in fines that had to be paid out have been forever enshrined in the public consciousness, one of the most interesting lessons from the disaster has largely been forgotten.

British Petroleum's disastrous oil spill highlights the dilemma organizations face when they fail to make the requisite crisis communications investments early—before they need them—and struggle to play catch up while the crisis fires (in this case literally) rage.

Reporters desperately sought information from any available source, and headlines critical of BP poured onto the web as fast as the oil spilling into the ocean. BP seemed incapable of responding at nearly every turn. They were simply not prepared. Perhaps the most visible example of their lack of preparation in the early days of the crisis was the brand hijacking undertaken by an anonymous source that launched what appeared to be a BP-branded public relations Twitter handle for the company: @BPglobalPR.

The account went live in May with a seemingly innocuous tweet, stating, *"We regretfully admit that something has happened off of the Gulf Coast. More to come."*

Unlike Johnson & Johnson's efforts to understand the potential risk from online trolls and brand hijackers, BP either ignored or missed the new account entirely, just as journalists hungry for regular updates began to follow it.

In less than a week, the account ballooned to over 25,000 followers, nearly five times the reach of the real BP account, @BP_America. In short order, the real intentions of this Twitter troll became clear as the account let loose a torrent of tweets, painting a picture of a remarkably out of touch company just as BP was struggling to regain its own narrative. Signs that something was either horribly amiss with BP's leadership team or that something more nefarious was underway appeared with this tweet: *"Please do NOT take or clean any oil you find on the beach. That is the property of British Petroleum and we WILL sue you."*

The outrageous nature of the post aside, media outlets picked it up and carried it far and wide with joyous frenzy. Was BP really this out of touch? Even when the media caught on, tweets from the troll spilled forth rapidly (though BP had still yet to comment on the account):

> "You know what they say about the ocean.... Once it goes black it never goes back! JOKING—the water is brown."

> "The ocean looks just a bit slimmer today. Dressing it in black really did the trick! #bpcares"

> "Catastrophe is a strong word, let's all agree to call it a whoopsie daisy."

The company had failed to make the basic investments in crisis monitoring in advance of their moment in the spotlight. They failed to recognize the potential brand hijacking threats posed by social media. In the process, they not only became the poster child for the worst environmental disaster in years, but their response efforts became a laughingstock.

By June, @BPglobalPR had over 150,000 followers—absolutely dwarfing BP's real account. After three weeks of vitriolic tweets, BP finally succeeded in having the account labeled "fake" according to Twitter's guidelines for parody. But the damage was done, and the incident has become a cautionary tale in public relations history.

Considerations for Every Crisis Response

The benefit of developing a crisis communications plan during peacetime is that it forces tough conversations internally—conversations organizations need to have now before an actual crisis unfolds. Take the time to think through your likely crisis scenarios and have honest conversations with your team about the weaknesses and vulnerabilities in your system.

Before you find yourself knee-deep in a crisis with a mile-long list of things you wish you had done to prepare, consider the following questions now, during your peacetime.

Do you have a proactive crisis communications plan?

Remember that a crisis communications plan is as vital as a firefighter's tools. Your chances of surviving a crisis with your reputation intact are far greater with a well-planned and practiced strategy in place ahead of time. If your organization has failed to develop an initial plan, doing so is priority number one. A survey of more than 500 companies found that fewer than half had a crisis communications plan in place. Far fewer had a digital crisis plan. Don't be caught off-guard without the tools needed to survive and even rise triumphant from a reputation catastrophe.

If you have the resources available, bringing in an outside crisis counselor to offer perspective and support developing your plan can be immensely helpful. However, don't let the absence of funds keep you from doing, at a minimum, a self-assessment and internal audit of current capabilities and foreseeable needs.

Who is on your crisis management team?

Designate an internal lead responsible for managing the crisis response and identify other internal stakeholders. Legal, compliance, marketing, communications, customer service, corporate security, and IT all may need to have a seat at the crisis management table. A lot fewer hands tend to be raised to volunteer when the alarm bells are ringing. Crisis management cannot be the collateral duty of all and the responsibility of none. Make sure your team has invested the time to understand the individual roles and responsibilities each brings to the table. It is never a good idea for your crisis team members to meet each other for the first time in an actual war room scenario.

Identifying and empowering the leader and the supporting team before the inevitable power-grabs, infighting and face-saving efforts collide to complicate clear ownership of the situation during an actual crisis, will ensure the team is ready to swing into action when the moment arrives.

Are you equipped to respond to a crisis on social media?

The most effective crisis assessment efforts include thorough social and digital media audits of each brand or external-facing organizational entity. Besides protecting the integrity of the brand, these efforts ensure that appropriate channels have already been established where reputational threats are likely to occur. That preparation equips the response team to act quickly when the fire alarm rings. X, Facebook, LinkedIn and YouTube are considered the primary channels today. However, platforms such as Instagram, Snapchat, and TikTok can also be appropriate for crisis response, depending on where your detractors decide to wage war.

An effective audit will not only identify the response channels needed but will, as we saw with Tylenol, uncover what others are already saying about your brand. Take action to prevent any hijacking of critical accounts or protected internal messaging, and talk about how you would respond online if a crisis started to erupt.

Ask yourself:

- If a video crisis were to emerge, how quickly could a video response be posted?
- Does your organization have a video camera or other recording equipment?
- Is there a teleprompter available or a business relationship with a trusted vendor who will be responsive?
- Is someone monitoring the corporate reputation online 24/7, or are they simply pushing out marketing efforts?
- Who (if anyone) on the internal crisis team would have immediate access to the corporate X or other social media accounts?

Now answer the above questions assuming you need to respond after-hours or on a weekend. How about on a holiday? Would your brand bleed out for twenty-four to forty-eight hours in the court of public opinion, or would you be able to respond quickly to stop the bleeding?

If your organization has spent years building a carefully massaged brand channel to discuss all the benefits of your product or your organization, you might not want to forever pollute that stream with the negative commentary that will come your way in a crisis response effort. You may wish to consider moving that conversation to another account—perhaps a corporate account or a customer service-focused X handle. The average Fortune 500 company today operates multiple X accounts for precisely this reason; one size rarely fits all when it comes to a winning crisis response.

Is your website ready?

Moving beyond social channels, a good digital crisis response plan will consider the need to identify locations on the organization's website for a corporate blog or other long-form content where a letter from the CEO or Frequently Asked Questions could be posted during a crisis. Short-form tweets can be great for rapid-fire responses, but they are rarely enough to communicate nuanced messaging with the level of depth needed to calm rising public anxiety.

Getting legal approval to establish a blog on a Sunday in the middle of a holiday weekend can take hours, if not days, away from the critical response efforts. And that doesn't even address the IT and web development resources that might be required to actually build the site. Building the platforms now, before they are needed, and establishing the appropriate internal rules for posting during a crisis will save time and streamline response efforts when time becomes the most precious commodity

How will you respond to public inquiries?

For larger organizations, taking the time to create call center and customer service crisis response procedures can eliminate significant headaches later down the line. In a data breach or other consumer recall, the potential numbers of those impacted can rapidly jump to hundreds of thousands and millions. Phone lines will be overwhelmed. Organizations lacking an internal call center should use this time to identify an outsourced call center service and negotiate a contract that can be activated without additional legal review the moment a crisis occurs, allowing for seamless processing of the inbound inquiries.

When a crisis hits, reporters and the public often turn to the organization at the center of the storm for information first. This will not only overwhelm the phone lines, but far too often can crash websites and other forms of digital communications. Good planning efforts will include working with the IT department to determine the ability to flex bandwidth capacity in a crisis and establish back-up plans allowing for surge capacity should the need arise.

One final note on being prepared: Production quality is not necessarily as important as the quality of the actual content. An iPhone video with a simple five-dollar tripod and a twenty-dollar microphone can often fit the bill. If the CEO is not available, there are likely other appropriate and caring voices to shepherd the message. Don't let the search for perfection prevent you from taking the steps necessary to save your reputation.

The list of peacetime activities could fill another twenty pages and, while it is important to have a complete checklist of activities and considerations, that is not the purpose of this book; that is the purpose of your actual crisis plan. The primary purpose of this book is to ensure you understand the full spectrum of crisis possibilities and embrace the right habits and mindsets for preparing, responding, and recovering appropriately. Check your crisis plan against the situations covered in this book and ascertain whether all possibilities have been considered.

In Part II, we will study the science of crisis fires and learn how to respond skillfully to adapt to an ever-changing landscape.

Machiavelli's advice remains as true today as it was 500 years ago. Use your peacetime wisely to understand your likely risks, identify internal ownership, develop the right plan, and make the strategic investments necessary to be prepared to effectively respond to the next crisis. The costs of failing to prepare will far outweigh the costs of investing in making ready now.

PART II

On the Crisis Frontlines

N o matter how well you prepare, no matter how sound your plan may be, when you find yourself on the frontlines of a crisis, responding appropriately is an equal mix of art and science. Like having a child—but much less rewarding—there is only so much you can do to be ready for an event that *will* turn your life upside down. I know from experience, however, that certain missteps could be fatal to your reputation, while other actions can help to steer through to eventual victory. In Part II, several case studies that illustrate the most vital dos and don'ts will be presented to equip you to act and remain poised for a strong recovery.

CHAPTER 10
REMAIN CALM

*"Only the unprepared are
overcome by pressure."*

-Lou Holtz

n 2004, during my time serving President George W. Bush as a spokesperson for the US Ambassador to Iraq, I had a front-row seat witnessing one of the purest examples imaginable of remaining calm under pressure. This was a tense time for the recently liberated nation as militia forces within the country mobilized to deny the Iraqi people a free and democratic society once again. One of my responsibilities was to manage the visits of major network news figures to the country. Mobility within Iraq was difficult and the networks relied on the military to provide safe transportation and access to the frontlines. In late March of 2004, as the insurgent uprisings began in full force, I was tapped as point man for legendary reporter and journalist Dan Rather's week-long stay in Iraq for the CBS Evening News. Upon meeting this icon of American media, I was instantly struck by how incredibly polite and engaging he was with everyone he met. He stopped to personally thank every soldier we passed for their service. It was a gesture that he sincerely meant. The week was a success and we agreed to cap it off with an interview with Ambassador Paul Bremer, the man leading the multinational coalition effort to rebuild Iraq and transfer sovereignty back to its government.

As the hour approached for the interview, I joined my security detail for a quick ride into Baghdad's Red Zone to pick up Rather from his hotel and escort him back to the relatively safe confines of the Green Zone and Republican Palace to meet the ambassador. The Republican Palace had been one of Saddam Hussein's primary residences, and in an odd twist of fate it became the Coalition's headquarters for rebuilding the nation he had so neglected.

We picked Rather up a little after 6:30 p.m. on what was turning out to be a cold evening in the "land between two rivers." We cleared the fortress-like security to re-enter the safety of the Green Zone and then entered a second level of security to gain access to the Republican Palace, as the time for the interview was rapidly approaching.

At a few minutes past 7:30 p.m., the ambassador and the news anchor settled into their seats, microphones on, lights lit for the exclusive interview that would shape global coverage of the progress in Iraq for the next week. For the first few minutes, everything went as planned. Unfortunately, that was usually about when things hit the fan in Iraq. And "hit" they did.

From out of nowhere, we first heard, and then felt, several loud thuds. I checked my watch to see if it was at the top of the hour, when the military conducted regular controlled explosions of confiscated weapons. Unfortunately, it was half past.

A few moments later, the attack alarm began to sound, roaring like the World War II blitzkrieg sirens in London. The ambassador didn't miss a beat. He continued answering Rather's question. The seasoned newsman asked a second question. Everyone remained calm and collected. As the alarms continued to ring, Rather leaned in and politely asked on camera if there was anything "we should be worried about." Bremer replied, showing an equal amount of calm and resolve, that if they needed to move, people would be in shortly.

Not thirty seconds later, a swarm of security forces swept in and literally lifted the ambassador off his feet, ushering him to a secure location. The compound was under an insurgent rocket-propelled grenade attack. My own security detail was still with us and the lead agent, a former special operations warrior himself, quickly checked his hand mic, assessing the situation. The CBS crew was chomping at the bit to chase down Ambassador Bremer and "get a shot" of him heading into his bunker or any footage of people running into the attack shelters. Our security leader reported that an unspecified number of rockets were landing in the Green Zone, and that while we were under direct attack, the best thing we could do was to sit tight in the secure room we were currently in. To Rather's credit, he turned to his six eager crew members and told them to stand down and relax. That was the end of that discussion.

After what seemed like an eternity, the all-clear signal rang out and the ambassador returned for the final portions of the interview. Everyone was a bit tense, and as Rather began his first question, a loud cell phone began to ring. We frantically looked around for the source of the audio-killing ring, but to no avail. A bit sheepishly, Bremer slipped his phone out of his pocket and turned it off. It was the perfect ice-breaker moment, and we all enjoyed a good laugh.

When your crisis situation comes, it will feel like bombs are literally dropping all around you. Your instincts will urge you to move faster and make quicker, less thoughtful decisions. In short, you will be tempted to lose your calm and your perspective. Just as Bremer knew he needed to remain composed as the camera rolled and just as Rather knew he could take his time to get the story he needed on his terms, in a crisis you cannot allow the situation to dictate your actions. Not every incident is a crisis. Knowing how to discern a true crisis from unpleasant news articles, a nasty tweet, a tough earnings cycle, or a routine product glitch can often be as important as responding effectively to a truly devastating situation.

Crises crave structure. They demand perspective. Any leader can run around like Chicken Little stating the obvious. The most effective crisis managers are the coolest cats in the room during the darkest hours. The calmness they exude assures those around them that the situation is well in hand—even if the sky really is falling.

CHAPTER 11

BE WHERE YOUR CRISIS IS

"Half the battle is showing up."

-Stephen Hawking

On Easter Sunday of 2009, in the quiet little town of Conover, North Carolina, the actions of two fast food employees would soon set into motion one of the biggest corporate embarrassments of the year. The crisis event would become the foundation for countless business reports and communications case studies throughout the next decade.

While millions of families busied themselves with Easter egg hunts on what was surely a slow workday, two Domino's Pizza employees decided to fill the internet with a series of prank videos shot from the restaurant's kitchen, showing numerous disgusting acts carried out on the food being served to customers. The two employees filmed themselves putting cheese down their pants and up their nose, blowing snot onto pizzas, and acting out a litany of equally disgusting acts. The series of videos went viral globally, setting off a chain reaction that drained millions of dollars in lost profit from the pizza maker. Within days, millions of potential customers had viewed the videos, which dominated all online search results for the company.

The situation that was unfolding for the pizza maker would be a defining moment for the role of digital and social media in a crisis. In today's crisis situations, social and digital channels can play one of three roles—the match that lights the crisis fire, the oxygen that gives it fuel and, if done right, the extinguisher that puts out the flames. The initial role we see coming into play is that of the instigator. In this reality, social and digital channels become the match that ignites the crisis (such as with the challenges facing Israel's military). In this increasingly common situation, the very cause of the crisis stems from the massive scale of social connectivity today. This was the case for Domino's as well, which was about to face its biggest crisis moment in decades. The second, and by far most common role, is the accelerant, as we've already seen in several stories. The massive availability of always on and connected social channels to rapidly spread information has enabled what previously would have remained a small-scale or regionalized annoyance to explode virally, publicizing the embarrassment for all to see. In these instances, such as the challenges faced by IKEA, the crisis is not caused by the social channels; social media is simply the gasoline on the already-lit fire that fuels the news to greater heights. The third role social media can play is in extinguishing crisis fires. This is arguably the most important role, and one that will be covered in more depth in later chapters. This is where the deft use of real time social media engagements can outpace the spread of misinformation or circumvent biased media sources enabling your messaging to break through the way the Boston Police Department leaned in to correct misinformation and ultimately support their manhunt efforts.

During the first twenty-four hours of the pizza crisis, the videos sat online, undetected by Domino's as hundreds of thousands of viewers watched the disgusting acts being performed on pizzas then delivered to unsuspecting consumers. From the beginning, Domino's had failed to clear even the lowest bar of crisis preparedness covered in Part I: No one was listening online.

As the videos spread virally, Domino's remained oblivious to the threat until a blogger reached out to the company for comment. While Domino's flailed about in shock, the blogosphere sprang into action and the popular site *Consumerist* utilized clues in the videos to identify the franchise location—before the parent company did. Twenty-four hours later, the suspected employees were fired, but not before setting off a firestorm that Domino's was woefully unprepared to extinguish.

The company's initial response was to lawyer up and demand the videos be removed from YouTube due to copyright claims, a key misstep in a situation that demanded transparency and accountability. This was not an approach that put customer concerns first; this was a legal approach hoping to bury the news as quickly as possible, missing the fact that in today's world nothing is ever truly "removable."

According to *The New York Times*, when the company learned about the video on Tuesday, executives "decided not to respond aggressively, hoping the controversy would quiet down" on its own.

According to one executive, "What we missed was the perpetual mushroom effect of viral sensations." A company spokesperson would later tell a reporter that the chain would "not be posting statements on the company website for fear of alerting more consumers to a negative story." Millions had already watched the videos at that point. The Domino's team so misunderstood the landscape their crisis was playing out on that they simply didn't show up. By the time the company realized the depth of its crisis and organized itself to respond, they committed their next error: opting to respond via a press release to a crisis that was unfolding in a video medium. If, as Stephen Hawking suggests, half the battle is showing up, Domino's had already lost by failing to "show up" on the primary platform the crisis was unfolding on.

The company also had no Twitter account prior to this crisis. And despite the tens of thousands of tweets that were sharing the video, Domino's was unable to get one launched until the fourth day of the disaster.

It would ultimately take a full week for the company to post a response video, finally engaging within the YouTube universe where millions had already watched the vile acts of its employees.

Making Lemonade from Lemons

This story and its ending would be a typical one in the crisis annals if it were not for one key final, redeeming fact that saved the company from utter ruin: unlike far too many that stumble and never learn, the Easter Sunday videos served as a wake-up call for Domino's. The entire organization rallied around not only improving the quality of the pizza they served, but of dramatically scaling their technology and digital infrastructure. Today you can track your pizza from the moment it is ordered through the entire production chain, all the way to your doorstep.

While there can be no doubt that the company suffered financially in the immediate aftermath, Domino's stands today as one of the strongest players in the market. While the company failed the initial tests of "showing up," they quickly learned from their brush against the crisis fires and built the tools and connectivity necessary to mitigate future threats.

CHAPTER 12

FIRST, DO NO HARM

"It depends upon what the meaning of the word 'is' is. ... If it means there is none, that was a completely true statement."

–William Jefferson (Bill) Clinton

I f there is one absolute in the world of crisis communications, it is this: Much of what you think you know to be true in the early hours of a crisis will be tested. As your crisis moment unfolds, the principal responsibility of any crisis manager is to follow the same credo as physicians. Namely, job number one is to first do no further reputational harm to the patient.

Nothing can inflict greater pain into an already hurtful situation than the loss of credibility—the credibility necessary to combat the attacks you are weathering, and the credibility necessary to begin to reset and take control of your own narrative. And the absolute surest way to nuke your credibility is to release false information—whether intentionally or not.

This may seem like an obvious rule to follow. You know you need to be honest and forthright with your stakeholder audiences. You know you want to remain on the moral high ground. Why, then, do so many fall prey to dealing in misinformation or out-right falsehoods? This chapter introduces a twist that may feel jarring to some after unpacking the lessons covered to this point. Here is the twist: sometimes the best thing you can do to extinguish the crisis fires burning around you is to deny them oxygen.

Responding in the Dark

The urgency to respond, to answer the hordes of incoming questions, and to reassure the concerned can be overpowering in a crisis. You will be urged by every corner, by every external audience—including friends and family and neighbors—to "say something," to "refute the charges," or to "set the record straight" on specific allegations. The pressure to "do something" will be enormous.

A key challenge in the initial hours and days after a crisis is that you simply will not have all the information at your disposal—and much of what you believe to be solid information will ultimately become less so with time and additional due diligence. The public won't give you credit for trying to be responsive if the information you give turns out to be false. They will simply assume you either don't know what is going on, and thus have no ability to solve the problem, or that you deliberately misled them, and thus everything you say going forward will be shrouded in doubt. This is where the critical balancing act comes into play between engagement to correct the arch of your crisis moment and temperance to wait for more complete situational awareness.

This was the tough lesson meted out to British Petroleum back in 2010. As BP's crisis began unfolding, reporters were desperately seeking information from any available source. As has been noted previously, BP's failures in the early hours and days of the oil leak to effectively manage the crisis could fill entire volumes on their own. What ultimately sealed their fate from a reputational perspective was that they allowed themselves, and their messaging, to be driven by the crisis rather than taking control of the situation and establishing their own cadence of engagement. Hour by hour, and press conference after press conference, BP attempted to push out what they believed to be the latest information about the severity of the leak and their containment efforts. As each announcement came, almost like clockwork, independent sources countered the information and BP found itself continuously having to recall their findings or expand upon their analysis at each subsequent media engagement—and each time, the update was worse.

By allowing the crisis to dictate the response, they found themselves regularly having to recall incorrect information to a point where few believed the company actually knew what was going on or was capable of fixing the problem. At each turn, BP deepened their reputational chasm.

The lesson here is a hard one because it can appear to pit two key pillars of effective crisis response against one another: the need to tell your story and avoid an information vacuum, and the need to not speak too soon or incorrectly. The "just right" response in between these two extremes is to assure the public, as soon as possible, that you are aware of the situation and are working constantly to understand and rectify any potential errors or mistakes immediately. If you don't know an answer, own it. If you think you know an answer but cannot be sure, caveat it. And critically, when you blow it and get information wrong, be the first to correct the record as quickly as possible and take responsibility for your mistakes.

In a crisis, the public wants to know, more than anything, that you know what has caused the problem and that you are working to fix it. They care less for the nitty gritty details about how much oil is still leaking out or how long it will take to fix. They assume if you have identified the cause, you can identify the cure. They will keep this assumption for as long as you keep a covenant of honesty and transparency with them.

There is one last point to address as you consider your crisis move, and that is the "twist" noted earlier. Sometimes, the best path forward is to simply take your licks and remain quiet, hoping that the speed at which today's modern media cycle evolves will quickly move past you. This is one of the most difficult decisions a crisis team will face. Failing to engage on a story that ultimately spirals forward without corrective action could seal an individual or organization's fate as a bad actor in the court of public opinion. At the same time, there are instances where the crisis is not burning as hot as those in the immediate vicinity may think (or feel) it is.

Sometimes Less Is More

Just as dangerous as responding too soon is ignoring how the situation appears from the public's point of view. Regardless of the truth or your intentions, you need to take into account public perceptions of the truth as you consider how to respond. Otherwise, their perceptions will be written into history as the reality.

Earlier in my career, a client was facing withering critiques for alleged sexual encounters. The individual was being accused of having consensual sexual relations outside of marriage and was adamant that no such encounters had ever happened. After hours of preparation and questioning, we felt fairly confident in our position and began putting together a strong campaign to push back against what our client was telling us was a false and damaging narrative.

As we prepared to wrap up, the client paused, looked up, and said, "Oh, there is one more thing I should tell you. While we never had sex, I was naked with [the person]." Game over. From our client's perspective, the charges being leveled were absolutely false and the initial denial was an honest attempt to counter the allegations. However, clearly, in the court of public opinion, a complete denial would never hold water and would destroy any credibility the individual may have had going forward. The decision was made to avoid engaging in the back-and-forth and let the dust settle. Sometimes the best way to survive a crisis fire is to avoid giving it any oxygen and let it burn itself out.

Just as Bill Clinton's semantic quibble about what "is" is failed to impress the grand jury during his testimony about his affair with Monica Lewinsky, any skirting around the whole and complete truth will come back to haunt you. If you are left explaining in a crisis, you are usually losing. The public is exceedingly forgiving for those who seek absolution. They are equally resolute in their feelings toward purveyors of falsehoods. Everyone loves contrition. The public will crucify you for lying, but will just as quickly champion you for falling down and asking for forgiveness.

Don't destroy your credibility by rushing out half-truths or unverified information or attempting to mislead. You can never get back your credibility, and it is the one thing you will need more than anything to survive the crisis waters.

CHAPTER 13

HUG YOUR LAWYER (OFTEN)

"I'm trusting in the Lord and a good lawyer."

–Oliver North

The crisis communications credo referenced in the previous chapter—to first do no harm to what is left of your reputation—was introduced to help shape awareness of the risks associated with inflicting unnecessary damage through poor crisis response programs.

This credo is important for many reasons, but perhaps the most important is this: By embracing this mantra early, the seeds are planted to build critical alignment between the communication and legal teams necessary to drive a successful response strategy. Holding true to the credo relaxes the natural tension that exists between communicators and lawyers, and enables both teams of experts to function at their highest performance. Teams that don't embrace the credo often find that their first adversaries are the colleagues sitting across the table.

Throughout my time in crisis war rooms, I have lost track of how many senior communication professionals fancied themselves armchair legal experts. Unfortunately, just as many general counsels have also believed they wrote the book on smart public relations. The reality is that both sides likely have just enough experience working with the other to be dangerous. Both come to the crisis table wary of the risks each could introduce to an already tense situation.

For the communicator, the urge will be to run around the legal team, convinced that all good ideas die in the general counsel's inbox. The urge to act now and ask for forgiveness later has led to far too many PR debacles. For the legal beagles, the urge to clamp down, say nothing, and do nothing that could potentially make the situation worse will be overpowering. All of their legal training tells them to be risk averse and to never "ask a question you do not already know the answer to."

Keith Rudduck, the former general counsel for Royal Dutch Shell, who had faced several headline crises during his quarter-century legal career adroitly captures the natural tension that exists between arguably the two most critical players in a crisis. "Lawyers are generally trained to avoid, or at least minimize, legal risks and exposure to the greatest extent possible and typically tend to look to long-term consequences," writes Rudduck. He continued: "However, in a crisis situation, adopting a legalistic approach may only serve to worsen the outcome."

Partnering Successfully with Legal

The realty in a crisis is that the natural push and pull between the legal and communication team can be a healthy exercise, as the best approach typically sits somewhere between the two extremes. A crisis is neither the time for aggressive risk taking nor for overly conservative silence. Finding the happy medium will be near impossible if trust does not already exist between these two teams.

"Lawyers face a difficult dilemma when responding to crisis situations," says Shell's Ruddock. "Adopting too legalistic an approach may lead to response paralysis and increase negative reputational impact. Yet too light a touch may create major future legal exposures. Nonetheless, I believe that lawyers need to focus pragmatically, rather than legally, on what is required in the short term to minimize long-term exposure. If lawyers take their role of protecting the company from any legal exposure in a crisis situation too far, they may (eventually) win the legal case, but could well have already lost the reputational argument. Most companies can withstand a major financial impact, but a reputational disaster will take years to recover from."

Ruddock's approach is one hardened during some of the biggest oil and gas crises of the last quarter century. While the regularity with which he faced reputational risks most certainly helped build the muscle memory and trust between the two teams, the same success can be found in communications efforts much sooner if certain ground rules and relationships are established prior to a crisis.

During my time at one of the leading crisis management agencies, I helped manage a major reputational threat for a global pharmaceutical company. No industry in the world is more heavily regulated on what and how they may engage the public than the pharmaceutical market. News was about to break about a significant product liability issue, and our team knew we needed to help shape the conversation, rather than allow competitors, analysts, and opposition groups to determine the storyline.

From a legal perspective, there was almost no benefit to engaging in the court of public opinion. The lawyers were confident that the company was right in its actions (as they ultimately were proven to be) and that any engagement risked maligning the legal strategy. The challenge we were presented with, however, was clear: There might not be a customer base left for the product if we did not assuage public concerns and ensure fair and accurate reporting carried the day.

Because I had spent significant time working with companies in the healthcare space prior to this campaign, I was able to engage the legal team in asking the question "What can we do," rather than declaring, "Here is what we want to do." We knew, for example, that this story would be widely shared on social media. We also knew that any form of real-time communication and response system was impossible, given US Food and Drug Administration (FDA) regulations on marketing communications.

Working with the legal team, we developed a fairly robust arsenal of pre-approved statements, tweets, and a blog post that addressed the core concerns we anticipated would drive the media cycle. The responses were not as tightly spun as the communication team would have liked, tending at times to tilt toward the bland grey zone of legal-approved commentary. That was not the point. The point here was to move the ball from the legal team's safe zone of refusing to say or do anything to mid-field, where we would have room to fight for a draw in the court of public opinion.

By engaging the lawyers early, the communication team was able to make the case directly that they not only shared a belief to do no harm to the brand, but that they also understood the regulatory and legal minefield that any communications needed to traverse. The trust that was built at the beginning released the "pucker factor" for the legal team and enabled both sides to work collaboratively on common ground.

As with any partnership, the crisis management team's ability to work together with the legal team is a relationship built on trust. Once that trust is eroded, it is very hard to rebuild. Avoid the urge to "act first and ask for forgiveness second" in a crisis. Your crisis play will have many acts. You don't want to take one of your most important players off the stage permanently by losing their trust for a small tactical win.

Partnerships Must Be Two-Ways

While the primary purpose of this chapter was designed to instill the value of working closely with legal counsel in times of crisis, it is important to provide a closing thought on why this relationship must be a partnership equals. A lawyer's job is to avoid risk at all costs, hence the favorite use of the term "no comment." From a legal perspective, no risk can come from no comment. The crisis manager's job on the other hand is to ensure whatever is left after the fire burns itself out is still viable. These two world views can, and often do, clash in spectacular ways. Winning in the court of law but being obliterated in the court of public opinion is the truest sense of a pyrrhic victory.

For a textbook case highlighting the risks of legal over-reach, we need only look to December of 2023 and to what *Politico* called "one of the most disastrous public relations moments in history."

By all accounts, the December 2023 congressional testimony by the three presidents of MIT, Harvard, and the University of Pennsylvania about the rising concerns of antisemitism on America's premier college campuses should have been straight forward. While the topic of antisemitism can be particularly rife with risk, the reality is that 95 percent of the answers to any anticipated questions should have easily fallen within a clear "black and white" spectrum of opposing all forms of hate, anywhere, at any time, in any form. Rather than a cakewalk, the hearing became a masterclass moment for how terribly things can go awry when the well-honed instincts of the legal team to "say nothing that could welcome risk" take precedent over all other considerations.

Congress was calling these leaders of higher education before the cameras, and the American people, for the great theatre that is a congressional hearing with the precise goal of hoping to show just how "out of touch" elite universities had become. The narrative they wanted to achieve was set. It was clear and it was widely known. For anyone preparing to raise their right hand and sit for the theatrics of a hearing one fact must remain paramount during preparation: you are being hauled in as a prop to support the divergent agendas of the elected officials who are each vying for a thirty second sound-bite on cable news and a quick clip to share across social media hoping for a moment of virality that will help their cause, raise more money for their campaign or capture new voters. No one is looking for a dialogue. The goal of anyone testifying is simple: do not become the story. As Chris Armstrong, a partner at one of Washington's preeminent lobbying firms Holland & Knight has counseled, "When helping a client prepare for a congressional hearing, the goal is usually to help them perform in a way that is knowledgeable, respectful, and, ultimately, forgettable." In other words, you're not in the arena looking for a win, you're looking for a draw.

The problem the trifecta of university presidents faced on this particular day was they all appeared to be briefed by the same legal team terrified of answering any questions that could expose the institutions to legal risk. The back and forth between lawmakers pressing the three witnesses to condemn the call for genocide on their campuses, and their unwillingness to do so, became the exact viral moment the conservative committee chair was hoping for. DC power lobbyist Bruce Mehlman summed up the cause of the slow-motion car wreck that the hearing became stating "It seems to me they prepared for a legal proceeding and found themselves in a political environment bringing a knife to a gunfight."

Within days major donors of all three universities were threatening a halt to funding. Calls for the presidents firings or resignations mounted (two would ultimately lose their jobs within weeks). The fallout from "avoiding anything that could create legal risk" was laid bare for all to see.

The legal prescription was, by all accounts, far worse than the sickness. Legal and communications are the core "yin and yang" to a crisis team. To maximize the good of both, their authority and their impact must be empowered to balance one another.

CHAPTER 14

GET AHEAD OF THE STORY

*"Next to doing the right thing, the
most important thing is to let people
know you are doing the right thing."*

–John D. Rockefeller

n 2007, just as Twitter was transforming the 24/7 news cycle into the 1440 news cycle, Netflix was instigating a similar disruption in the TV media space. From the eighties to the mid-2010s, Americans had relied upon cable service to access hundreds of channels of content. Cable operators were the gatekeepers of new content. But, like CNN's innovative move to combine satellite and cable in the 1980s, Netflix's conversion from DVD rentals by mail to streaming-only services opened an entirely new medium for content providers. By 2024, the number of Americans who still watched television by traditional cable dropped from 76 percent in 2015 to less than half, and that number is expected to continue to decline as younger generations consistently look to streaming services to satisfy their entertainment needs. These cord-cutters (and cord-nevers) have reshaped the media landscape and, in the process, upended the old business dynamics between cable TV operators and content owners. Streaming platforms, the Rokus and Amazons of the world, are now positioned as the new gatekeepers to content.

The brave new content world these platforms have ushered in has been a hard pill for some of the old guard studios to swallow. After all, they just migrated out of a world where cable companies set the terms for distribution and they had little interest in replacing one gatekeeper for another. The third decade of the twenty-first Century is witnessing the new frontier of the streaming wars as a new era of "carriage battles"—disputes between studios and streaming services for the rights to "carry" certain content—takes shape. Apple, Amazon, Samsung, Google, and Roku have all faced challenging negotiations with studio owners feeling liberated from the old ways of distribution. Many of these content owners have no interest in sharing any of their revenue—let alone a fair amount—with the new platforms that enable their distribution. For many, this is a zero-sum game, where every dollar given away to a distribution agreement is seen as a dollar lost.

Some players—Disney is one that stands out—took very different approaches that embraced the new dynamic of the streaming world. Disney leaned in heavily with their platform partners, understanding the power they bring to building massive audiences. Disney's stunning success in achieving its five-year subscription goal in less than fourteen months highlights the value of this thinking. Needless to say, Disney's all-in engagement strategy for the launch of Disney+ was not the norm. The "all for me, none for thee" approach still reigns in the minds of many throughout the media and entertainment landscape.

In the spring of 2020, just as the world was shuttering its doors as the coronavirus pandemic took hold, NBC Universal was preparing to launch its new streaming service, Peacock. During this time, I was leading communications for the Roku platform. As the months ticked down to the launch of NBC's much-hyped streaming service, one very big partner was missing from its distribution: Roku.

As America's #1 streaming platform, Roku was a critical partner for any service hoping to achieve scale. A veteran of cable and content skirmishes, the team at NBC Universal and their parent company Comcast were preparing to dust off the old carriage battle playbook they had so effectively wielded in the past half century to force deal terms on Roku that were significantly beneficial to the legacy broadcaster. We saw it coming.

One lesson I have learned from both representing and facing off against big companies, big governments, big unions, and frankly, "big" anything, is that big does not always mean savvy or creative when it comes to a public dispute. These organizations will often hew to the well-worn path that got them to where they are today. In your own environment you will likely find that the antagonists you may face, including everyone from union organizers to critical NGOs like the Environmental Working Group, usually fall back on "what has worked before" as they plan their assaults. One group I encountered during my crisis agency days would post the same study every single year, on the same date even, decrying the safety of sunscreen. We could predict the month and week the attack would come annually because it came at that same time, every year, for nearly a decade. The "rinse and repeat" method deployed by these organizations creates a huge opportunity for any crisis manager to prepare for and mitigate the risk of such a threat so obviously seen through the tea leaves of the past.

Returning to Peacock, after months of negotiation, it became increasingly clear that NBC and its parent company Comcast had no interest in reaching a mutually beneficial agreement. The zero-sum game was afoot, and that meant only one thing: The old carriage warrior was readying for their usual assault. Unfortunately for Comcast, what they had not realized was just how dramatically different the battlefield of 2020 looked from the carriage wars of the past decades. The media conglomerate threatened to take several of its other apps off Roku's platform if Roku didn't accept what they believed to be unfair terms for hosting the new streaming app. Knowing full well the blame-and-shame playbook (blame the distributor for the removal of the apps, and shame them for harming the consumer), Roku simply stepped out in front and took the story directly to consumers, before NBC Universal or Comcast could spin the narrative in their favor.

At 4:00 a.m. on Friday, September 18 (because all crises happen on Friday), Roku leaders conducted dozens of back-to-back interviews with every major media outlet, detailing the unfair practices of NBC Universal and the detrimental impact they would have on consumers and their rights to access content on their platforms of choice. The reporters were all given the same embargo time to break their stories. At 6:30 a.m., the dam burst with a flurry of headlines calling into question NBC's tactics. Roku's statement at the time was designed to tell a comprehensive story of greed, unfairness, and anti-consumer engagement that any American who had ever had to call their local cable company for customer support would readily relate to.

Roku's executive said, "Comcast is removing the channels in order to try to force Roku to distribute its new Peacock service on unreasonable terms. Comcast has declined our extension offer and so far has also refused fair and equitable business terms for the distribution of Peacock—despite the fact that they stand to generate hundreds of millions of dollars in advertising revenue from its distribution on the Roku platform."

The speed with which the news dropped stunned NBC. Their tried-and-true battle plan hadn't survived even the first volley on this new media battlefield. Consumer response was swift and predictable; no one likes a greedy player. By moving first and with total engagement, Roku established the media narrative on its terms, and on hour one. Within hours, NBC Universal returned to the deal table they had walked away from only days earlier, convinced their playbook would work. They signed the Roku agreement without a single change. The new era of streaming carriage wars had begun and a new playbook, one that focuses on the consumer and on reaching mutually beneficial deals, had won the day.

The lesson here reaches far beyond the battlefield of today's multi-billion dollar streaming wars. If at all possible, don't let others tell your story. If, through your listening efforts or your business dealings you discover a threat is imminent—the best strategy I have found is usually to assume the high ground on the PR battlefield and lean in first on the offensive. This is not an easy decision to make, nor is it one to be taken lightly. While big companies are not necessarily savvy or quick to respond, it is equally true that, given time, they will be able to turn their battleship around and address you with the full force of their might.

When a decision is made to take the fight, the gloves must come off and the intestinal fortitude must be present to withstand the likely response.

The goal with the negotiations with NBC and Comcast was not to annihilate the company. In fact, the goal was to force the cable operator to realize that the rules of engagement had fundamentally changed and that there was a better way forward for both companies. While annihilation was not on the agenda, total message control was. Roku ensured every single media outlet that mattered was reached and offered access before Comcast had even woken up. Social media was carefully monitored and customers were directly communicated with. The totality of the effort left no ember alight.

When seeking to out-maneuver an opponent, it is far better to gain the first-mover advantage by getting ahead of the story rather than being caught behind.

CHAPTER 15
INOCULATE IN ADVANCE

"My attitude is that if you push me towards something that you think is a weakness, then I will turn that perceived weakness into a strength."

–Michael Jordan

Robert F. Kennedy was fond of saying that one of the best approaches to confronting difficult challenges was to "hang a lantern on your problem." In other words, to shine a light onto one's perceived weaknesses first, before others can frame the debate.

In his fantastic book (and a must-read for any student of effective communications) *Hardball: How Politics Is Played, Told by One who Knows the Game*, author Chris Matthews sheds further light on the power of "hanging a lantern" on your problem. Matthews writes "When you put your problems right up on the table, it is a sign of strength and it allows people to move past it much more easily. Also, if you appear weaker, you can receive a David and Goliath type sympathy and people will root for you as the underdog."

I like to take RFK's concept of "hanging a lantern on your problem" one degree further to not only shining a light onto the issue, but, much like Michael Jordan, reframing it entirely from a potential threat to a source of differentiated strength.

The art of "inoculating in advance" is one of the most powerful tools in the crisis avoidance toolkit as it recognizes and then neutralizes (or inoculates against) potential threats before they can spread. Ronald Reagan's 1984 debate quip for example that he would "not make age an issue of this campaign," and was not "going to exploit for political purposes my opponent's youth and inexperience" so completely disarmed the Democratic nominee Senator Walter Mondale that even he could not help burst out laughing. Reagan had masterfully inoculated in advance of the very likely attack that age was a disqualifying factor in the campaign. While political histories are filled with similar stories, there are also numerous practical examples of the power of inoculation.

In the mid 2010's, I was advising Ford Motor Company as the automaker prepared to release an entirely new design for its #1 selling pickup truck, the F-150. While many may conjure images of the iconic Mustang when hearing the Ford name, it is the F-150 that has become the Detroit mainstays bread and butter, with the company's stock rising or falling on the success of this one vehicle.

Given the singular importance of the F-150, Ford knew that nearly any change, no matter how small, would receive significant attention. And in the model year that lay ahead,

Ford was planning changes that were nothing short of revolutionary. The new F-150 body would be made of aluminum. This highly advanced material would deliver significantly greater fuel efficiency at a time when gas prices were becoming pocketbook concerns for consumers.

While Ford engineers marched forward with their game-changing design, the marketing team recognized this innovative new approach could be ripe for competitor attacks. Internal consumer polling showed that when asked about aluminum, most potential buyers thought of beer cans or of the tube of Reynolds Wrap in their cupboard. These were not the rough and tumble off-roading workhorse of a truck images Ford wanted consumers focused on.

Given the highly competitive truck market, we knew for certain that the team at General Motors would stoke the "soda can" narrative to its full advantage. There was no hiding from aluminum; it was the central evolutionary shift under way. Instead, we needed to reframe the entire concept of aluminum and inoculate ahead of any potential threats.

Our outside consulting group comprised several former political and campaign hacks, and together, we leaned into a novel approach. We were going to run a "political campaign" reframing our aluminum into the space age, military-grade aluminum that it was. We would take our "campaign" to every rodeo, county fair and NASCAR race in the country. We would show the military's use of aluminum in armored vehicles and highlight NASA's use of it in space—all designed to send a clear message: This stuff was tough as hell.

By the time the launch came, Ford had fully inoculated against the potential risks from competitors attacking aluminum. If it was tough enough for the army and advanced enough for space, it was good enough for your driveway.

The new Ford F-150 launched without disruption retaining its place as the #1 truck sold in America.

You will not always have the opportunity to hang RFK's "lantern" on your problem before those seeking to do you harm strike. Even when potential risks are identified, robust internal debates will occur about the likelihood of these risks ever seeing the light of day. The hope is always that perhaps in this case, the critical information will remain secret, staying outside of the public view.

These are tough calculations and there can be no absolute admonishment as to the right or wrong course to take without a full picture of each individual situation. However, one north star should guide these deliberations: ask your team and yourself how much better off you or your organization would be if you had the opportunity to frame the bad news on your terms first, rather than being placed on the defense by those seeking to twist the knife even deeper.

CHAPTER 16

COMBAT MISINFORMATION WITH AGGRESSIVE TRUTH-TELLING

"A lie can travel half-way around the world while the truth is putting on its shoes."

–Mark Twain (falsely attributed)

For some crisis moments, there is no warning. Natural disasters, investigative reporting, employee missteps, and state-sponsored cyber-terrorist data breaches have all had headline-grabbing turns at the crisis wheel in recent years. In these situations, there truly was no opportunity to "be first." Sometimes, despite your best efforts, a story will get out in front of you, leaving you stuck playing defense against a torrent of misconceptions.

On the afternoon of Friday, March 11, 2011, just such a moment occurred on the island nation of Japan as it was struck by the largest recorded earthquake in its history. The massive 9.1 magnitude "megathrust" earthquake unleashed a chain of events that would claim the lives of thousands, cause billions of dollars in damage, and set the stage for a global environmental catastrophe.

Just after the quake, the Japanese coastal population began bracing for the next wave of disaster. The Tōhoku earthquake had triggered a tsunami, sending 133-foot waves across more than 2000 kilometers of coastline. Situated along the coast for easy access to the necessary cooling waters for its reactor was the Fukushima Daiichi nuclear facility and it now found itself directly in the eye of the coming storm.

Nearly an hour after the initial quake rocked the nation, the tsunami waves breached the reactor's seawall, leading to an explosion that was captured on video and shared virally around the world. The single greatest nuclear disaster since Chernobyl in 1986 was unfolding live on television and streaming on the web.

The extraordinary access to visual images—the reactor exploding in real time on camera—made it the hottest news story in the world. That footage was slowed and analyzed thousands of times by media commentators. As events began to unfold, the Nuclear Energy Industry's crisis war room sprang into action. The NEI represents nuclear companies and, while this reactor accident was not caused by one of their member companies, they had a significant stake in this crisis. The reputational fallout for the NEI, which had worked so hard to rebuild trust with the American people following the meltdown of a nuclear reactor at Three Mile

Island in Pennsylvania nearly forty years earlier, was a real and immediate threat.

This was the first large-scale nuclear disaster in the digital age and the first one to fall within the 1440 news cycle. Within hours of the reactor explosion, I found myself in NEI's crisis war room, helping manage a nuclear PR crisis as we established a first-of-its-kind digital response team. This story was already being told on YouTube, Facebook, and Twitter, and we had to act fast to maintain the trust and reliability NEI had so painstakingly built over decades.

Misinformation was traveling at breakneck speed and being given credibility by the mainstream media. Rumors flew in a never-ending frenzy to fill airtime with "new information," relying less on vetted sources and more on "who had new information of any kind to share." Local reporters in California trying to capture the public's attention fanned out to Toyota car lots with Geiger counters, testing the radioactivity of cars on the lots—an act patently absurd when you realize that the cars had been sitting on the lots for weeks or even months before the disaster struck Fukushima.

Reporters from major networks were deployed to farming communities in California to report on the safety of the water being used to water the grass that the cows were eating. The fear of the moment stated that nuclear-tainted waters from Japan were reaching the California coastline. One heading blared: "Is Our Milk Safe?" Anti-nuclear blogs and other activist social sites began promulgating fake news articles, claiming everything from the meat we ate to the milk we drank and the air we were breathing was contaminated, despite the FDA's public findings to the contrary.

The old way of doing things—hosting a regular press conference and providing updates as they were available—would not stem the tide. The lies were traveling faster than the truth. The crisis response team had one clear objective: Every half-truth or piece of misinformation needed to be combatted with science. And we needed to engage in the mediums in which the hysteria was fomenting. Dispatching a press release or hosting a TV news conference would not reach the Twittersphere or the millions of people who consumed snackable news via short YouTube clips.

Changing the Tide

To engage quickly and effectively, the NEI established a video response team that interviewed nuclear scientists and safety experts in real time to address rumors with videos that could be rapidly posted and shared. High-end production value was not the goal; speed and accuracy were paramount. As these videos posted, news outlets began calling, asking to have the subject matter experts live on their own networks, a major win for the industry that was working to calm anxiety with real science. Recognizing that Twitter had become the new assignment editor for reporters seeking real-time information, the NEI launched the @NEIupdates Twitter account and directed reporters to follow it for instant updates. They also launched the "NEI Nuclear Notes" blog to provide longer form content updates in addition to the new YouTube channel.

Tens of thousands of readers turned to the blog for detailed scientific answers. Thankfully, in anticipation of public interest, the NEI also immediately secured additional web bandwidth, understanding that the industry's reputation would further suffer should its own website crash from the crush of people seeking information.

The NEI's efforts would ultimately be rewarded. Filling the vacuum of misinformation with facts, responding in the mediums where the debate was happening, and operating at the speed the media now required made the difference for the nuclear industry.

In the immediate aftermath of the earthquake in Japan, seven out of ten Americans were concerned about the chance of a nuclear disaster in the US. Just one month later, following the aggressive truth-telling efforts by the industry, a Gallup poll in April 2011 revealed that most Americans once again believed US nuclear facilities were safe.

In a crisis of any magnitude, you cannot allow others to tell your story. The media has a job to do, whether you like it or not, and in today's intensely competitive and highly opinioned newsrooms, sitting out doesn't mean that your story won't be told. It simply means someone else will tell it for you.

CHAPTER 17

TELL THEM, TELL THEM, AND TELL THEM AGAIN

*"Content doesn't win.
Optimized content wins."*

–Liana Evans

For years during my corporate career in the public relations agency business I challenged those around me that were developing incredible content to embrace the rule of three. The principle is simple: If you are developing a piece of content—be it a video, an infographic, a great picture, a blog post, anything—develop a plan to optimize it at least three times. This principle takes on even more urgency in a crisis situation where time is of the essence, and you will not have the ability to constantly develop enough fresh content necessary to feed the 1440 news cycle.

In practical purposes, the rule of three looks something like this: If you have taken the time to write a blog post, publish a bylined article, or conduct a media interview, consider how to repurpose the content you worked so hard to develop and get legal approval for. Look for ways to leverage your content across all your owned and operated channels in order to reach more of your stakeholders who will be looking for information during a crisis. Think about ways to transform the original content into other modalities. For example, clip short highlights from an interview or a blog post into a series of tweets or Instagram posts. Link the same content to your Facebook and LinkedIn accounts. Consider shooting a ninety-second video with the author or the thought leader and then upload it to YouTube and share it on social media.

Unlike Kevin Costner's *Field of Dreams*, in a crisis, if you build it, it doesn't necessarily mean they will come. Audiences are bombarded today with thousands of pieces of content. To make sure your messages break through, you need to not only build them—you need to market them.

Use the re-purposed content to pitch reporters who likely didn't see your engagement efforts the first, second, or in many cases, the third or fourth times. In a crisis, it is natural to feel like your audience is paying rapt attention to your every move. For you, it is the biggest news event of the day. But, for most everyone else, it is one of a thousand points being sprayed at them across the most fragmented media landscape in the history of human civilization.

It will be important to realize that, in fact, the world is still moving forward and that unless your nuclear reactor just exploded or your cruise ship ran aground and is slowly sinking on live television, most of the world isn't paying attention to your crisis or your response efforts. Around 2300 years later, the best piece of advice for effectively communicating to any audience remains the same as when Aristotle first delivered it: "Tell them what you are going to tell them; Tell them; And then tell them what you have told them." The third time you have delivered the message will likely be the first time anyone has heard it.

Don't Forget Your Paid Strategy

I will end this chapter with an important call out for optimizing content during the development of any effective crisis strategy. You cannot assume your audience is actively refreshing your webpage or stalking your social feeds for the latest information you are sharing. What we can assume, however, is that when people learn of a crisis or hear bits of concerning information from friends or the nightly news, they will act as they have been trained to do for the past two decades.

Ask yourself this question: Where do you first go for immediate answers to questions you have, be they easy cooking recipes, the weather, or help diagnosing your latest ailment? That's right, Google. And in a crisis, Google searches related to your organization or brand or to you personally will skyrocket. In times of a product recall, worried consumers will turn first not to their trusted medical professionals for advice, but to their search engine asking, "Is X safe?" If they hear of a data breach, before calling the credit card customer service line, they will ask Google, "How do I find out if my data was breached?" and so on and so forth.

And just as this pattern of human reaction has played out with certainty time and time again, it is also a reality that there is only one way to best Google's carefully guarded algorithm for search to ensure content lands at the very top of every Google search in real time: You need to buy it.

William Shakespeare's reminder to all of us, embedded in the second scene of the second act in *The Merry Wives of Windsor* that "if money go before, all ways do lie open" serves as a wonderful reminder of the importance of utilizing every arrow in the crisis quiver to shape public perception during a reputational threat.

The tactic is known as negative keyword optimization, and while this book is not specifically intended as a tactical guide for crisis response or search optimization, in this instance it helps to illustrate the broader importance of combining paid and earned strategies in a crisis. Most major brands today have robust search engine marketing campaigns in place, buying every possible consumer search term designed to drive sales (for example, "what's the best car/hotel/restaurant"). Few, however, take the time to also invest in capturing the *negative* key terms their audiences may be searching for in a crisis. During one crisis for a global consumer products company, we recognized that concerned consumers would flood Google seeking information about the product. We also knew that many of the sensational news headlines about the crisis would organically rise to the top of Google search results because of the credibility the search engine provides "news" content.

During one thirty-minute session, the crisis team brought in a cross section of employees and asked them to write out how they would go about searching for the information. Dozens of keywords and phrases such as "is the product safe" and "where can I return my product" were identified. A small campaign was launched to "buy" all those phrases across Google. Since no one was likely going to be competing for these terms other than plaintiff-trolling trial lawyers, the cost would be relatively inexpensive. What the data showed was incredibly powerful. More than one-third of those who searched for the potentially damaging content during the crisis clicked through to the company's messaging at the top as part of the sponsored keyword campaign rather than clicking through to the sensational media stories.

Combining paid and earned strategies into one effort designed to fully optimize messaging and break through the clutter that concerned consumers might be reading, helped the crisis moment to pass even more quickly. Similar strategies can be deployed in traditional print, across X and Instagram and even with YouTube. As with the rule of three, you need to ensure your messaging is everywhere. In a crisis, don't hesitate to combine your paid and earned components together.

CHAPTER 18

PEOPLE OVER LOGOS

"A picture is worth a thousand words."

–Henrik Ibsen

A s you work to make sure your message is heard amidst the chaos of social media, one key piece of advice will help ensure your voice breaks through the din. This is a lesson already hinted at in earlier situations covered: In times of crisis, people want to hear from humans, not faceless organizations or ChatGPT powered AI bots.

Several years ago I was invited by a senior Russian businessman to Moscow to present on effective crisis communications to a quarterly gathering of business leaders. As I prepared for my presentation, I reviewed relevant case studies in the region and the social media practices of many of the most visible people and businesses in the country.

Now, when I present to audiences around the world, I still share one finding I uncovered from my research more than a decade ago that serves as an important lesson for those seeking to win trust and secure reputations in today's socially connected world.

At the time, Dmitry Medvedev was serving as the president of Russia. He was a younger leader brought in to broaden the appeal of Russia's actual leader, Vladimir Putin. Medvedev, leaning into the social channels of the day, had established two personal profiles on Twitter—one in Russian and one in English to help advance his public relations objectives.

The Kremlin had also established two accounts, again with one in Russian and the other in English. President Medvedev's account was branded as his personal account.

Messages were regularly written in the first person, implying a real human was posting the content. The account would cover breaking news, personal insights on culturally relevant sporting events, and select global events. The Kremlin account, by contrast, read as if it was being auto-generated by a 1980s-era teletype computer. The impact was clear. Despite posting 20 percent less content than the official Kremlin accounts, Medvedev's personal account had amassed five times as many followers. The universal message, whether in Russian, English, or any other language, is that humans want to interact with other humans, not logos. This basic human instinct becomes even more transparent in times of crisis.

As you establish, or as you review, your social media accounts, consider giving them a real voice. This is the primary reason why so many organizations today operate several accounts on the same platforms. Each account should establish unique channels for unique conversations. If you have a complaint or an urgent matter, these forward-leaning organizations want you to take that to their customer service account where real humans, and in many cases increasingly sophisticated AI-powered vetting services, are monitoring and responding in real time (AI can be very helpful in a crisis but still cannot fully replace the power of human touch). Many will even list the names and often show the pictures of the social media team right on the page, allowing a concerned customer to see who is taking the time to help address their concern.

For some organizations, having a human face may simply be a non-starter. If you find yourself in this situation, take the time to think differently about your "corporate face." Have you given your social accounts a unique "voice" that authentically connects your brand with your followers? Moving beyond simple broadcast messages to developing channels designed to engage in a dialogue will be key to your response efforts when the crisis hits.

Show Some Personality

During the first few days of 2017, burger maker Wendy's Twitter account exploded on the scene in an incredibly refreshing and positive way for the brand that serves as a great case study for how to humanize an organization's voice on social. The Twitter account, which stated: "We like our tweets the same way we like our fries: hot, crispy, and better than anyone expects from a fast-food restaurant," had been active for more than half a decade posting and replying to comments from the community with little fanfare or notice.

On January 3, 2017, however, Wendy's "brought the sass" as one headline proclaimed, to its response to criticism that its burgers were indeed frozen, not fresh, as their multimillion-dollar marketing campaign had claimed. This was a direct assault on the company's signature brand promise in the market. Here is how the now-infamous exchange went down:

@Wendy's: Our beef is way too cool to ever be frozen

@NHride: Your beef is frozen and we all know it. Y'all know we laugh at your slogan "fresh, never frozen" right? Like you're really a joke.

@Wendy's: Sorry to hear you think that! But you're wrong, we've only ever used fresh beef since we were founded in 1969.

@NHride: So you deliver it raw on a hot truck?

@Wendy's: Where do you store cold things that aren't frozen?

@NHride: Y'all should give up. @McDonalds got you guys beat with the dope ass breakfast.

@Wendy's: You don't have to bring them into this just because you forgot refrigerators existed for a second there.

The Twittersphere erupted with laughter. The popular online news site *Mashable* called the exchange and the many that would follow in the days ahead an "unexpected beacon of light" showing us "that brands have the potential to do so much more" with their social media account. In the case of

Wendy's, they decided to give their Twitter account a personality and they unleashed that personality in an authentic, funny, and engaging way.

As the snappy exchange gained popularity, Wendy's head of marketing shared that "the intent of the social media team is to represent the brand's voice as best as they can." In Wendy's case, they gave life to a logo in a way that empowered the company to both respond to criticism and proactively promote the brand authentically.

Humans are fairly predictable. We want to interact with other humans. In a crisis, we want to know a caring individual is on the other side of the phone line, the tweet, or the Facebook post.

CHAPTER 19

HUMOR'S DOUBLE-EDGED SWORD

"Funny is a good foil. Humor is illuminating, and it also gives you power."

–J. Tillman

There is a fine line to walk in any attempt to be more human and relatable. As the previous chapter outlined, we instinctively want to engage with others on more personal levels when we are in times of need. One of the most personal and humanizing traits is humor. When your crisis moment comes and you are seeking a path across what may seem like unnavigable waters, humor can be equally effective in both building bridges and in burning them.

No one would ever risk suggesting there is anything funny about anti-Semitism. Nazism even less so. So, if you happen to be a consumer-facing company whose ad campaign accidentally went viral because of its perceived resemblance to Hitler delivering his infamous salute, you are absolutely not laughing.

Unfortunately for discount retailer JCPenney, this is exactly the situation they found themselves in when an advertising campaign for a new tea kettle erupted across social media channels in May 2013. The JCPenney case is a classic example of when social media played the role of "accelerant" for a crisis. In a world before everyone was connected at the hip with a digital device, the uproar over the JCPenney ads would never have seen the light of day. But in 2013, with the snap of a camera and just a few swipes on the screen, the world was able to see for itself the "Hitler Tea Kettle" in all its glory.

In reality, the Hitler comparisons were a major stretch, as you can see from the side-by-side images. Nonetheless, the story was erupting on social media. The team at JCPenney faced a clear moment of truth. Which course should the 100-year-old retailer take? Do they ignore the brewing debate online or dive right in? Do they pull the ad campaign down, or do they push full steam ahead? Do they wait to see if the threat grows into a full-blown crisis when anti-defamation groups and investors like George Soros, who had just invested billions into the company, were demanding action? The story jumped the Atlantic, moving from California, where the billboard was first spotted, to the United Kingdom where *The Telegraph* headlined: "Kettle that looks like Hitler brews trouble for JCPenney."

In JCPenney's case, the team took a deep breath and had the perspective to see just how ridiculous the attacks were. No one could claim with credibility that the company had in any way acted with malice. Still, they knew not to ignore the situation entirely. The company decided to switch the narrative and point out the ridiculous nature of the commentary with a little humor of its own.

Instead of getting defensive, the brand replied to tweets with variations of the message, "If we had designed it to look like something, we would have gone with a snowman or something fun."

As JCPenney looked to make "some lemonade" from the media cycle with which they had been gifted, the kettle went viral within twenty-four hours and sold out that very afternoon. JCPenney's clever handling of the kettle conundrum not only allowed the crisis to blow over, it actually led to an increase in the company's sales. However, in order to avoid any further offense, the company wisely decided to remove the kettle from its site, as well as the billboard where it was first spotted. This decision showed that JCPenney could laugh about its mistake but also take the initiative to right any perceived wrong or violations of broader shared norms.

The Risk of Misusing Humor

Not every crisis moment calls for a laugh. In fact, most will not. Blogger Karl Vaters in 2020 offered a wonderful five-step blueprint to follow before choosing to deploy humor in a time of crisis.

First, Vaters rightly guides us to run any thought of attempted humor by someone else. Humor has an incredibly strange way of landing differently based on culture, upbringing, or life experiences. What is funny to one can be horribly offensive to another. To avoid doing any further harm, ensure the attempt at humor is actually funny for the masses.

Second, Vaters says to "laugh with, not at." Humor can work, but it can be most powerful when it is either self-effacing or avoids criticisms of others. If you are tempted to use humor to take down someone else in a crisis, it is probably the wrong time to use it.

Third, keep it lighthearted, not edgy. As we saw with the Wendy's response, the humor was good-natured and fun. It managed to call out the fallacy of the argument against the company without being personal or aggressive. In fact, the even-keeled banter made you want to root for Wendy's.

Fourth, use it to instruct. This is perhaps my favorite rule of the five. Returning again to the Wendy's example, humor was used to make the case clearly for how they can have fresh, never frozen burgers. Delivering truth with a smile will endear audiences to your cause in a crisis and show that if you are smiling and taking the higher road, you must have nothing to hide.

Finally, the last rule Vaters points out is a cautionary one. If you're not sure, don't post it. Don't risk the potential benefit of landing the humor correctly if you have any inkling it could land poorly. The potential for good is not outweighed by the likely risk.

Feel free to use humor, if appropriate and with discretion. Above all, keep the crisis credo in mind when deciding your messaging: First, do no harm.

CHAPTER 20

DON'T BECOME THE VILLAIN

"In time of crisis, people want to know that you care, more than they care what you know."

–Will Rogers

At some point in your crisis scenario, you may find yourself between a rock and a hard place, forced to choose between what appears at first to be saving your reputation versus protecting the public. The stakes will be high regardless of which of the seemingly only two paths you see before you: self-preservation or self-sacrifice? If you make the wrong choice, it will set the tone for the rest of your crisis encounter and make recovery more difficult—if even possible.

This scenario regularly plays out in issues of product recalls and data breaches—two forms of crises that tend to generate intense media scrutiny and that usually impact large swaths of the public. Let me share two examples to highlight the risks and the rewards that can follow from making the right or wrong call when your moment of truth arrives.

The Right Call

In October of 1982—long before the Infant's Tylenol safety cap or the Twitter takeover discussed in previous chapters—Johnson & Johnson's Tylenol was at the center of one of the biggest corporate crises ever. Media outlets began reporting that cyanide-laced Tylenol capsules had been found in the Chicago area and were linked to several deaths.

To understand the significance of this threat to the brand, one must remember just how big, and important, Tylenol was to J&J in 1982. Tylenol was the dominant market leader, capturing greater market share than its three closest competitors combined. Sales of the pain reliever accounted for nearly a third of the parent company's annual revenues.

The story of how the cyanide may have gotten into the capsules (still unsolved forty years later) and the ensuing media coverage has become one of the most retold crisis studies in America.

According to a *Fortune* magazine cover story following the crisis, "as the story started to break, even more calls began to pour in from pharmacies, doctors, hospitals, poison control centers, and hundreds of panicked consumers, many asking for clarifications J&J couldn't give, and many others making what turned out to be false reports of possible poisonings."

David E. Collins, chairman of McNeil Consumer Products, the makers of Tylenol, recalled that "It looked like the plague. We had no idea where it would end. And the only information we had was that we didn't know what was going on."

In crises of this magnitude, when the public is concerned and the media is demanding answers you don't have, your next move will shape and define how all of your following actions are viewed. Will you be seen as acting in good faith, putting the public before profits? Or will you be seen acting with self-interest?

While the details of the crisis and Johnson & Johnson's response efforts remain relevant to this day, what ultimately allowed J&J to rebuild trust—rapidly—had less to do with how it recalled the product and the development of its new tamper-proof bottle, and more to do with the direction the company's chairman set for his team from day one. Chairman James Burke asked his team to focus on two questions, in this order: First "How do we protect the people?" And second "How do we save this product?"

The company's decision to recall every product on the shelf despite there being no evidence of a widespread contamination was driven by a focus on protecting the public. It served to remind the public that J&J was a victim here, too—someone had tampered with their product to do evil and Tylenol was going to do everything it could to remove the threat. It was a difficult choice—but it was the right choice.

J&J reminded the public that this was the result of an outside actor, and that the company was working with law enforcement while doing everything it could to not only remove every product from the shelves, but to also develop new safety measures for the future. Tylenol remained in the "victim" boat with the rest of us, not the villain boat with the bad actors who had actually conducted the crime. The company and the brand emerged from the crisis stronger for having acted in the interest of the public.

The Wrong Call

Not every leader is as forward-looking as J&J's Burke. As we discussed previously, in today's highly litigious environment, too often the legal team envelopes and suffocates good crisis response efforts in the interest of "avoiding exposure." This understandable reaction leads to decisions that, upon public reflection, appear to have been taken to protect the company at the expense of the public. At the time, the decisions are rationalized. "We don't have all of the answers" is an oft-heard refrain in a crisis war room (or, as Starbucks's CEO said, "There is no playbook") used to argue against transparent engagement during a crisis.

On November 27, 2013, Target faced just such a moment. In the days following Black Friday, the retail giant's security personnel discovered a sensitive data breach had been carried out against their credit card system. This data breach occurred during the most critical time of the year for the retailer, as holiday shopping accounts for the lion's share of their annual sales. It also occurred during a particularly sensitive time for consumers who rely upon their debit and credit cards for travel, purchases, gifts, and other expenses during the holidays.

In a data breach, as with most product recalls, companies have a brief window to make a critical decision: Do you put the interest of the public first, or do you try to contain the news as long as possible and hope against hope that it never becomes public? We will discuss data breaches further in the next chapter. In far too many instances, the urge to hunker down prevails. This was the case with Target. For three weeks, Target customers' data was exposed with no cardholder notifications from the company. News of this breach, however, would not be contained.

Less than a month later, on December 18, an online news outlet discovered the potential breach and reported their findings, prompting the US Secret Service to open an investigation. The following day, Target acknowledged that some data may have been compromised. Over the course of the next several weeks, a steady "drip, drip, drip" of new information and revelations came forth. As the number of impacted consumers grew by the *tens of millions* with each new announcement, the real-time impact to Target's bottom line became dire. Sales at Target dropped demonstrably in the final week of holiday shopping.

The lead paragraph of the *Forbes* story on Target's Q4 earnings tells us everything we need to know about the dangers of becoming the villain when in fact you were a victim of a criminal breach. *Forbes* wrote:

> The nightmare before Christmas—the credit card data breach that spilled information

on as many as 110 million Target customers—hasn't yet reached its final chapter. As
customers seek to regain confidence in one
of the nation's largest retailers, Target itself
is still paying a hefty price for the breach:
its profits fell nearly 50% in its fourth fiscal
quarter of 2013 and declined by more than a
third for all of 2013.

The hits kept coming. Target's CEO was eventually
forced to testify before a US Senate committee and then lost
his job under pressure for the company's mishandling of the
breach. Customers were furious. Because the breach had been
unreported for so long, many credit card companies began
canceling and reissuing cards to consumers—many of whom
were now on holiday travel, unable to access the new cards
waiting in their mailboxes and stranded with now-useless
pieces of plastic in their wallets. For those consumers, Target
sat squarely in the villain's boat.

Target and Johnson & Johnson provide bookended
cautionary tales for us all. The urge to hunker down, while
understandable, can be lethal. Just ask the Target CEO who
lost his job. The urge to push back against embracing responsibility will be immense. But the payoff for doing what is
right by the public when your moment of truth comes will
be just as powerful. Just ask Johnson & Johnson and their
billion-dollar brand Tylenol, which remains America's most
trusted pain reliever to this day.

CHAPTER 21

YOU ARE IN THE DATA BUSINESS

"Personal data is the new oil of the internet and the new currency of the digital world."

–Meglena Kuneva, European
Consumer Commissioner

I f you or your organization keep records of any kind of data—customer emails, credit card information, addresses, social security numbers, employee records—you are at risk of a breach. Even small businesses are not exempt from data espionage. Understanding that nearly everyone—every organization with a reputation worth defending—is in the data business today is an essential element of any effective crisis plan.

According to IBM's annual Cost of Data Breach Report, the average cost of a data breach in the United States in 2019 was more than $8,000,000 per incident. This is obviously an average that takes into account epic breaches that impact millions of consumers as well as smaller, more targeted breaches. The point, however, is clear. The cost of a data breach includes not only the reputation damage inherent in a crisis of this nature, but it also comes with real financial implications. As we move through the roaring 2020s decade of digital and online engagement, the number of data breaches and their representative costs have only accelerated.

In 2014, there were 783 data breaches reported, impacting an estimated 85 million consumer records. It seemed at the time we were hitting the high-water mark in breaches, as that number was already 500 percent higher than it had been just a decade earlier. In fact, it was just the tip of the iceberg. Over the next half decade, this number would explode in growth. In the first six months of 2019, more than 3,000 data breaches exposing more than 4 billion records were reported. There were likely thousands of additional breaches that were either never detected or never publicly reported. By 2023, the scale of data breaches expanded at a staggering rate. With just one breach, from what is almost hard to believe was a digital protection firm by the name of Darkbeam, nearly four billion records were exposed in one fell swoop.

Data breaches can take the form of everything from corporate espionage designed to siphon off competitor secrets to state-sponsored corporate raids from nations such as China and Russia that openly support the theft of American intellectual property. Breaches can come from the activities of well-funded and technically savvy international criminal organizations that profit from data theft as well as from simple hackers out to see what damage they can inflict. Data security threats can also result from simple negligence. The contractor who accidently provided access to millions of personal data files, for example, or the human resources officer who left a thumb drive containing all employee social security numbers at the local Starbucks, can be equally damaging to a reputation if managed poorly.

While it is easy to arm-chair quarterback the poor crisis response delivered by many who face a data breach, the primary lesson from this chapter is that you need to be ready for when that breach moment comes, regardless of how much planning, security, and oversight may be in place. This is a story Marriott learned all too well in 2018.

The Power of Remaining the Victim

In November 2018, Marriott reported in a press release what was, at the time, one of the largest data breaches in history. Personal information for approximately 500 million Marriott guests had been exposed. The core reputational challenge for Marriott was that this breach had occurred in 2014 and had only just been detected. The hackers, who were suspected to be working under the direction of the Chinese Ministry of State Security, managed to remain undetected for four years, quietly collecting data on millions of unsuspecting hotel guests right under Marriot's digital nose.

As federal investigators dug more deeply into the hack, it became clear that this was part of a multi-pronged intelligence-gathering effort of the communist government. This was not the result of Marriott's lapse in security or failed judgment. Marriott and its guests were the victims of a sophisticated cyber-attack.

According to *The New York Times*, which broke the Chinese connection, the Marriott database contained not only credit card information but passport data, which would be particularly valuable for tracking who is crossing borders, what they look like and how much time they have spent in particular areas. According to government officials, the Marriott hack was "only part of an aggressive operation whose centerpiece was the 2014 hacking into the Office of Personnel Management (OPM)."

The Chinese were working in a coordinated, multi-year effort to build detailed profiles on both potential spies and the Chinese nationals who were supporting them. According to *The Times*, the Marriott data married with the OPM data could then be used to track which Chinese citizens visited the same city, or hotel, as an American intelligence agent who was identified in data taken from the Office of Personnel Management.

In Marriott's case, it was the victim of a global espionage effort perpetrated by sophisticated Chinese state-backed hackers. There is likely very little the company could have done to defend against a coordinated attack that had also infiltrated the US government. The key in this instance, and in almost every major data breach, was to remain "the victim" in the eyes of the public and in the eyes of the specific consumers impacted by the breach. Marriott was attacked. It was robbed of data. Marriott along with those whose data was compromised, were all victims.

If a data breach is the result of a sophisticated attack, a criminal enterprise or other illegal activity, the best path forward is to not only remind the public of the source of the breach, but to embrace it. Your organization was victimized, just as the individual consumers were. You have all been attacked. You are all angry, and you are doing everything possible to right the wrong.

By reminding stakeholders first and foremost of your shared victimhood and your commitment to work with law enforcement to catch the bad guys, you begin your crisis response well-positioned on the moral high ground. You are not the bad guy. You did not cause this to happen. Don't forget this key advantage, and don't squander it by failing to keep the needs of the other victims paramount. Marriott had one key advantage in this breach incident: the villain's identity was not only believable, it was also far bigger and more powerful than Marriott.

This reality gave Marriott some much-needed air cover as, like Target, their initial reaction and notification was delayed by nearly eight weeks from their initial recognition of the breach. However, once they engaged publicly, they revealed what data had been compromised, offered an apology, and outlined the exact steps they were taking to address the situation. Marriott demonstrated its commitment to, and empathy for, its customers by establishing a dedicated website and call center to address questions and concerns, sending regular email communications to those affected, and providing a one-year subscription to a data protection service to all its guests.

It is typically in the initial hours and days of a breach that so many organizations fail to recognize the need to put the interests of those impacted above short-term concerns. The siren's call to say nothing, to avoid engaging because of the risk of legal action, and to hope it will "go away" has caused more reputational damage than nearly any other aspect of a breach. These instincts lead organizations to hesitate to invest in the forensic resources necessary to uncover how far and wide the breach is out of fear they will need to report it. The gripping fear that fuels inaction makes it impossible for those impacted to know how much of their data was lost and what they need to do next to protect themselves. At each step, if the organization only asked: "What would I want done to protect my personal data that had been breached?" and acted in a manner consistent with the answer, it would have remained firmly in the victim boat, viewed through the lens of an organization trying to respond to forces beyond its control. Marriott asked this question and acted accordingly; thus, they survived the crisis without losing customers' trust.

Unfortunately, more times than not, this is not what happens. Institutional inertia takes over. Legal concerns trump customer service goals. And before you know it, the media has turned the news cycle against you. The story has shifted from what happened, to when did you know and what did you do. In a matter of hours, you will move from victim to villain in the court of public opinion.

Preparing for Data Breaches

Every data breach is different. Some are criminal activities. Others are simply unfortunate accidents. However, in managing through several of the biggest breaches in the past twenty years, I have found that embracing the five following principles will best help to navigate the crisis waters.

First, never forget that the initial reports of the actual scope of the breach will likely be wildly inaccurate. The numbers will get worse because the gravity of what the forensic teams first uncover will worsen as they dig deeper. The numbers of actual users impacted will grow and so, too, will the types of data exposed by the breach. At first, it will just be the last four digits of the social security number. Then it will include birthdates and email addresses that were attached to a file you had not expected. Before you know it, mailing addresses and credit card numbers you had archived years ago were found on the server and also exposed. Each step in the investigation will pull you deeper into the rabbit hole and will likely uncover more potential damage. It is important that you and your team be mindful in the early days of a breach to avoid making definitive statements about what "has not" been compromised. Share only what you know (what you can confirm has been compromised)—not what you don't know. It will save you an enormous amount of grief in the eyes of the public down the road.

Second, regardless of what you may be hoping for, you do not control the timeline of a data breach becoming public. In response to the explosion of data breaches in the past decade, nearly every state in the country now has explicit laws regulating when and how consumers must be notified in the event their data is breached. This fifty-state patchwork has created a near impossible landscape to navigate for those without experienced legal counsel onboard. If you do not have legal counsel on staff now, identify a data expert to have available on call should you need to engage them. This will save critical time when the clock starts ticking. Many states require consumer notification within twenty-four hours of confirming their data has been breached. Significant civil and even criminal penalties can be levied for failing to meet these requirements. The clock is ticking the moment you detect it, and you likely have days, if not hours, to be ready to face the public. Have counsel ready and ensure your communications team is brought in during hour one to begin preparing for when the news breaks.

Third, working with law enforcement, while critical, is a double-edged sword. In the event you find yourself the victim of a criminal breach, working hand in hand with law enforcement is one of the best ways to reinforce the fact that you too are a victim and that you are doing everything you can to find the perpetrators responsible. Having the stand-by statement ready that details your work "together with local and federal law enforcement officials" is a powerful shield in the court of public opinion. Working with law enforcement can, however, also introduce new risks to your public relations strategy. The moment law enforcement is notified or involved, you lose all control over when, where, and how the information is delivered to the media. The FBI has entire press teams dedicated to media relations. Law enforcement has its own PR agenda and press strategies. Work with law enforcement, but recognize that for obvious reasons, protecting your reputation is not their top priority.

Fourth, be a good citizen. In a data breach, those who are impacted will be scared and confused. They will either have seen a news story that worries them, received an email notifying them they have been impacted, or worse yet, they may have had their credit cards limited or canceled as a rapid-response protocol from banking institutions wary of financial exposure from the hack. Your customers, members, employees, and supporters will want quick access to information that tells them if they are impacted and provides details on what to do next. One smart tactic is to establish an online portal directly enabling users to quickly confirm if they were impacted, as Marriott did. Just simply "knowing" will relieve a lot of tension. It is also a good practice to identify in advance a phone bank contractor to turn on quickly to manage a twenty-four-hour phone line to make it easy for those who are not digitally savvy to access information without having to wait on hold for hours. Utilizing X and other social media channels to push out updates as you have them also shows the kind of transparency that engenders good will. Email your customers with specific information so they first hear from you about what happened and what you are doing to protect them. Remember this simple rule: If your neighbor, someone you share a fence with or carpool within the morning, had their data breached and you were the first to discover it, how would you handle it?

Finally, remember that everyone will be scared. Everyone. In a data breach, organizations often focus their communications efforts on those impacted by the incident. And that is an important focus. What is often forgotten, however, are those not impacted.

Several years back, LinkedIn discovered a very small breach had occurred impacting less than 10 percent of its users. The company immediately notified those who were impacted and set in motion a process to protect their data. What LinkedIn failed to recognize, however, was that in a matter of minutes of their notification efforts, the entire world knew of the data breach. Media reports were flowing out. Posts on LinkedIn and other social sites began discussing it. Ten percent of LinkedIn's community felt comforted, because the company had reached out to and engaged them in a timely manner. But they didn't think to engage the rest of their community. Soon, emails and phone calls began flooding in and overwhelming the company. The emails and calls came from the other 90 percent of users who were now frothing with anger about what they perceived to be a lack of communication over a breach that could impact them. Remember, in a breach, *everyone* is scared. Be sure to have communication plans for everyone—those you know are impacted, those who might be, and even those you believe are not.

CHAPTER 22

THE C WORDS: CANCEL CULTURE

"Anyone who is suffering from shame and humiliation needs to know one thing: You can survive it... you can insist on a different ending to your story."

–Monica Lewinsky

The tumultuous 2010s saw not only the rise of data breaches, but the rise of a new threat in the crisis lexicon: cancel culture. Over the course of a few short years, from 2013 to 2018, these two words would come to describe the retaliation in store for nearly every form of transgression against a particular group, norm, or set of held values. From mundane moments accelerated by social media to truly horrible acts deserving of public rebuke (think Harvey Weinstein), to the more sensational "drive by" Twitter attacks that have destroyed the reputations of lesser-known individuals, cancel culture seems to be on the minds of nearly every individual with a reputation worth defending.

By the 2020s, we had reached a tipping point in the cancel culture wars, where many feared being canceled about as much as they feared being indicted by a grand jury.

Well-known YouTuber and cancel culture critic Natalie Wynn summed up the state of things in 2021 when she offered this observation: "It feels incredibly isolating, alienating, you feel incredibly angry because you feel that you've been deliberately misunderstood. There's a reason that public humiliation and exile have been used as punishment. In most societies, it really sort of triggers a lot of the worst social emotions that we're capable of feeling." When asked to define just how painful cancel culture can be, the sexual assault survivor didn't mince any words: "I was sexually assaulted by an acquaintance, these things are terribly painful to go through, of course, but what makes the canceling worse is that it's being done to you by people in your own community and you watch yourself be erased."

Attempted "erasings"—both big and small, impacting both the well-known and the unknown—have taken on a life of their own in some realms of the internet, fueling a self-propelling cycle of outrage.

In his 2021 column "How Everything Became Cancel Culture," author Derek Robertson traced the origins of cancel culture to an unsuspecting tweet that catalyzed and emboldened the outrage movement machine. According to Robertson, the "Patient Zero" for cancel culture was Justine Sacco. Sacco's story, and the dramatic shift in social norms it heralded, would ultimately impact nearly every aspect of our society, from celebrities to elected leaders, sports figures, and everyday Joes.

Patient Zero: Justine Sacco

Justine Sacco's story began on December 20, 2013, as the twenty-something public relations professional prepared to board a flight from London to Cape Town for a holiday. Sacco was a regular traveler, and her Twitter feed was dotted with quirky and at times off-color observations about her travels. She commented on the smelly passengers in first class and on the bad teeth and food choices of British travelers. None of those posts ever garnered much notice from her small following of less than 200. By all accounts, she was about as far away from being a social media influencer as one could be. Everything was about to change for her, however, as she boarded the eleven-hour flight to Cape Town and fired off one final missive into the Twittersphere: "Going to Africa. Hope I don't get AIDS. Just kidding. I'm white!"

Strapping in for the flight, Sacco fell asleep without a thought for the global firestorm she had just created. When she landed half a day later, she might as well have traveled to a different world. As the wheels touched down in Cape Town, she turned on her phone to reveal for the first time the nightmare she had unleashed with those twelve little words.

During the previous eleven hours, what one reporter had coined the modern day "digital lynch mob" had come for Sacco. The poorly worded attempt to highlight the racial disparity and the devastating impact AIDS has had on people of color in Africa had become irresistible chum in the water for the social media sharks. Sacco became the top trending topic on Twitter, with thousands of tweets calling for her head. Her employer soon responded as well, tweeting: "This is an outrageous, offensive comment. Employee in question currently unreachable on an intl flight."

Tasting blood, the mob dug at a feverish pace. "All I want for Christmas is to see @JustineSacco's face when her plane lands and she checks her inbox/voicemail," wrote one user. With pitchforks in hand, the assembled social masses leaned into the hashtag #HasJustineLandedYet, which then started to trend globally. The outrage machine had turned a tweet sent by an individual with less than 200 followers into a gladiatorial-style event with millions watching from the stands, waiting for the combatant to be torn to shreds by the lions as they cheered on gleefully. One Twitter user in Africa picked up the thread and traveled to the airport to capture an image of Sacco landing, which was quickly shared across social media with palpable euphoria.

Robertson called the entire incident a "moment when run-of-the-mill public shaming became a supercharged, social-media-driven process by which ideological norms are enforced." According to his article, "to beat up on Sacco wasn't simply to ruin the reputation of an individual human being who had made a mistake, it was to strike a blow for racial justice, putting Sacco's head on a pike."

Sacco's story, and the cancelings that have occurred in recent years, offer a cautionary tale for the speed at which the cancel train can barrel down the tracks. The sheer ferocity can be dizzying in today's connected media world. Nearly a decade ago, Sacco's reputation was utterly destroyed in less than twelve hours. Today, it can happen even faster.

And while these new forms of crises can burn hot and fast, it is also important to keep a healthy perspective that takes a step back from the sensationalism to demystify the true power of "cancel culture."

Navigating Cancel Culture

While these two words strike fear into the hearts of many, the reality is that those who have been "canceled" are few and far between in the grand scheme of things. Those who in hindsight were canceled unfairly are even fewer. Harvey Weinstein wasn't canceled. He was indicted and convicted. New York Governor Andrew Cuomo was not canceled. He was an accused habitual predator of women who was publicly held to account. No one today is mourning the frontpage loss of these individuals. Cancel culture and the social media infused dialogue that propelled their exit from the national stage was welcomed transparency and justice by many advocates for victims' rights.

The line we grapple with today is less about the extreme edges of cancel culture represented by Weinstein and his ilk, and more about the nuanced middle. How do you navigate a mistake you may have made or a statement from the past that in the light of today, in the here and now, is outside of current cultural norms? Are we no longer allowed, as either individuals or organizations, to make mistakes or to misspeak without the risk of a reputational death sentence? Are we as humans no longer expected to or championed for evolving our thinking, to learn and grow? And, importantly, should we stumble, how do we manage a crisis that burns so intensely hot?

Like most of the lessons from this book, the blueprint for these situations follows a similar path as many other crisis scenarios. To borrow the firefighting metaphor from earlier chapters, while each instigating moment of a canceling effort will feel unique, just as every fire has its own unique properties or causes for existence, the way they move, grow, and ultimately burn out follows a familiar pattern. Your goal in these intense and personally painful moments is to hold true to a few core guiding principles that have already been unpacked in this book.

First, and foremost, we begin with our crisis credo: Whatever your initial actions are, they must be guided by the principle that you *do no further harm*. Don't allow your response efforts to amplify the hate storm. This first rule may seem obvious, but too often, the initial reaction from someone being canceled only deepens the well of despair they will have to climb out of. When facing a mob of self-perpetuating resources, you cannot silence the noise with one ad hoc comment or X or Instagram post or press engagement. You will need a comprehensive strategy. Do not let your sense of urgency to "do something" quickly compound your situation.

Second: Don't allow yourself to give in to self-pity. There will be time for licking wounds later. That time is not right now. This rule can be one of the most difficult to embrace. YouTuber Wynn's commentary about the searing pain of being canceled makes it understandable that for many, the initial reaction is one of defense. Anger will soon give way to sadness. There will be a sense of feeling wronged and a desire to fight back. Those being cancelled want to immediately—desperately in some cases -explain why they have been wronged. The comments were from years ago, or they were out of context, or they never happened at all, or whatever the case may be, there will be an urgency to correct the record now. Those facing the judge, jury, and executioner of the social mob want "their day in court" to share how horribly painful it "feels" to be canceled in this way. While this is a perfectly natural instinct, it will only make the fire burn longer. No one is ready to attend your pity party just yet. Before you have "permission" to be a victim in the canceling play unfolding before you, you need to own your part in the drama.

Third: Listen first, speak second. Take the time to listen to the voices expressing outrage. Sort through the echo-chamber "bandwagoners" and find those who were actually hurt. Their words and insights will show you the path to redemption. Hidden among the tweets, emails, Instagram posts, Tik-Toks and Reddit threads that will come your way will be the words of those who were truly offended and hurt by whatever you are accused of having said or done. These are not the professional outragers, but those who have seen the coverage and are adding the context of their story and their experience to the narrative. Taking a beat to listen to these voices not only has the benefit of showing contrition and care, it will also help you understand more fully the road ahead. Be sure to take the time to listen before you speak.

Fourth: You need to own it. The sooner you turn the page to talking about what comes next, the sooner the fires will extinguish. This is where you begin to move into recovery. While your comments (or actions) may have been from two decades ago (or taken out of context), in today's light they may violate norms (assuming you have not broken any laws). It is okay to own that, and own it clearly. Share what you have learned during the ensuing years, how your own thinking and perceptions have evolved. If the issues were more recent, and you honestly were caught off guard by how they were perceived, own that too. You are not perfect. This crisis moment has given you a clarity that you are embarrassed you did not have before. Bring together what you learned from your listening efforts and embrace a commitment to continuing to evolve and learn and do better. We humans love a good rebirth story.

What we can't stand, however, is someone who won't accept responsibility. Richard Nixon was one of the twentieth century's most visibly "canceled" politicians. While Nixon never fully accepted the widely believed role he took in Watergate, his decision to resign was the ultimate act of "owning it." He turned the page and began to rebuild his reputation almost immediately. Within half a decade, just five short years after exiting the White House in disgrace, Gallup named Nixon one of the ten most admired people in the world. Everyone loves a comeback kid. No one likes a whiner.

Nixon's rebirth story also speaks to lesson five. Depending on just how bad your crisis is, you will likely need to make a sacrifice. For Nixon, it was resigning from the presidency in disgrace. For others, it may be conducting community service with an organization representing the issues you are entangled with. For still others, it may be a financial contribution to a non-profit to help bring about greater advancements. There are several ways to show personal sacrifice, and when the time comes, you will need to identify yours. Importantly, and again assuming the transgressions are not violations of laws but instead actions outside of the current established norms or accepted standards, the ultimate sacrifice doesn't have to be your career or your reputation.

The final step will sound familiar, as it is one this book has repeatedly highlighted. In nearly every situation, there will be an opportunity to at least try to make something good come from your crisis. Look for the moment to have something good come from both your pain and the pain of others. If you are going to be forced to go through the cancel culture crucible, seek the opportunity to not only come out of the storm a wiser or kinder or better-informed person, but also to have made a positive impact on the world around you. In the early hours and days of your cancel crisis, this will seem impossible, but trust that if you follow a clear path forward your opportunity will present itself.

In 2021, a highly visible celebrity whose team I was working with on a major production announcement went through the cancel culture wringer. Her experience offers helpful guideposts to benchmark as you navigate through the five steps outlined above.

A Case Study in Canceling

In May 2021, model and power influencer Chrissy Teigen was facing the biggest crisis of her career. Decade-old tweets had resurfaced of her appearing to bully model and media personality Courtney Stodden for her decision to marry a man nearly three times her age. In a series of tweets, Teigen was shown to have directed numerous comments many believed were encouraging the then-minor Stodden to commit suicide. For Teigen, these tweets played into a historical narrative filled with past missteps on social media. This time, however, the cancel mob mobilized and came for the star full force. Within days of the old tweets resurfacing, major contracts with Bloomingdales and Macy's were canceled. The former darling of social media was now its favorite foil. Unfortunately, Teigen's immediate reaction fell into the double trap outlined above of both doing more harm and embracing self-pity.

"Not a lot of people are lucky enough to be held accountable for all their past bullshit in front of the entire world," Teigen tweeted in the middle of the crisis. While completely understandable at a human level, the comments were interpreted by many as an attempt to highlight the pain she was feeling for being held accountable for her perceived cyberbullying of a teenager. No one was in the mood to listen to—let alone feel sorry for—her.

After her initial stumble out of the gate, Teigen thankfully recognized it was time to change course and implement step three. The social media star put down her phone, paused her Twitter account, and listened to the people her words and past actions had hurt. She did that over the course of the next month and embraced the kind of self-imposed social media exile necessary to remove oxygen from the cancel fire.

Teigen listened and then moved into step four, taking unequivocal ownership of her mistakes. She unabashedly offered herself as a case study to highlight the evils of cyberbullying and online trolling. She pointed to her past as a guide for young girls who are obsessed with social media as a warning for how not to behave. And then, much to her credit, she did the one thing most likely to reset her course going forward: She asked to be judged by what she did next.

In a long and heartfelt posting online, Teigen shared the following from her personal journey:

> As you know, a bunch of my old awful (awful, awful) tweets resurfaced. I'm truly ashamed of them.... There is simply no excuse for my past horrible tweets. My targets didn't deserve them. No one does. Many of them needed empathy, kindness, understanding and support, not my meanness masquerading as a kind of casual, edgy humor. I was a troll, full stop. And I am so sorry.

After owning her mistakes fully and without reservation, Teigen then began to turn the page and speak to the broader societal ills her actions reflected and why their toxic poison needs to be extracted from the public discourse. She wrote:

> In reality, I was insecure, immature and in a world where I thought I needed to impress strangers to be accepted. If there was a pop culture pile-on, I took to Twitter to try to gain attention and show off what I at the time believed was a crude, clever, harmless quip. I thought it made me cool and relatable if I poked fun at celebrities.... Now, confronted with some of the things that I said, I cringe to my core. Words have consequences and there are real people behind the Twitter handles I went after. I wasn't just attacking some random avatar, but hurting young women—some who were still girls—who had feelings.... There's no justification for my behavior. I'm not a victim here. The subjects of your sympathy—and mine—should be those I put down.

Before concluding, Teigen took the opportunity—an opportunity she earned by taking full responsibility at the beginning of her message for the gravity of the situation—to make it clear this is not who she is today:

> The truth is, I'm no longer the person who wrote those horrible things. I grew up, got

therapy, got married, had kids, got more therapy, experienced loss and pain, got more therapy and experienced more life.... My goal is to be so good that my kids will think this was all a fairy tale. Not the fake good. The good that has the best intentions, the good who wakes up wanting to make her friends, family, her team and fans as happy as possible. The good who will still fuck up in front of the world but rarely, and never not growing only more good from it.

She concluded with this closing thought: "I won't ask for your forgiveness, only your patience and tolerance. I ask that you allow me, as I promise to allow you, to own past mistakes and be given the opportunity to seek self-improvement and change."

The star, having laid her soul bare and said her piece, then went into a self-imposed summer away from the spotlight. Her words needed to sink in. Time needed to be given for healing. She challenged herself, and her followers, to judge her by what she does next. And, as a person who wants to forgive and see the phoenix rise from the ashes, she knew this was her best shot forward.

Within four months, the canceling seemed to fade. Teigen and her celebrity husband John Legend hosted a Democratic party fundraiser for five of the more prominent members of the US Senate—Cory Booker, Amy Klobuchar, Alex Padilla, Gary Peters, and Ron Wyden—who, by this time, were all clearly comfortable associating with and being hosted by

Teigen. Several weeks later she conducted her first televised interview since the scandal broke. Her comments reflected on the journey through cancel culture that is possible when you truly commit to owning your mistakes and bettering yourself in the process. Sitting with *TODAY* host Hoda Kotb, Teigen shared: "There's this whole cliché, 'I'm glad it happened,' but the reality is it truly made me a stronger person, a better person." Within months she would be standing on stage in New York City, no longer the pariah, attending the advertising industry's biggest streaming event, the NewFronts, with the team from The Roku Channel announcing the second season of her show *Chrissy's Court*. The announcement had been postponed for months and ultimately could have potentially been shelved entirely had the title star taken a different crisis redemption path forward.

In true crisis form, as I was preparing to submit the final copy of *Communicating Under Fire* for publication another major crisis moment gripped the world. This time, it didn't involve a social media posting from a celebrity influencer. No, this time it involved one of the most famous actors in the world and it played out on live television being watched in hundreds of millions of homes globally. The Will Smith, "slap heard round the world" incident offers another sharp reminder for how to manage a breathtakingly stupid and self-inflicted crisis moment. Just as with Teigen, the entire Smith team mismanaged the initial moments of his assault. The arrogance of the celebrity was on full display, right on down to the tweet sent by one of Smith's children addressing the assault stating, "That's how we do it." For a man who should have been celebrating the achievement of a lifetime, Smith was facing searing criticism from all quarters and even the potential of criminal charges. His initial statement fell flat as he failed to acknowledge the victim and own his actions. He was, as is cautioned above to avoid, doing more harm than good.

The narrative needed to be altered and quickly. Humility needed to be injected into the court of public opinion before they rendered a verdict against one of their favorite celebrities. As the media frenzy intensified with a guessing game about what possible punishments would come Smith's way, the actor and his team finally course corrected and got out in front of the story. Smith released a full-throated apology and owned his mistakes. He then preempted the Academy's own review process and offered up a sacrifice. He resigned from the Academy of his peers. Then, he went into exile quietly, letting the dust settle. The crisis embers continued to burn for a while longer but the fire itself had largely been extinguished. Nine months after the slap incident Smith would headline the opening of *Emancipation* in theatres in December of 2022. While the movie was a financial failure, his reemergence back into the Hollywood fold was well underway with new movies slated for release in 2024 and 2025.

Canceling is brutal—of that there can be no doubt. To hear one victim assert her experience as worse than her own sexual assault gives vivid color to just how painful and stigmatizing it can be. However, it does not have to be fatal.

CHAPTER 23

IN A LAYOFF, DON'T LOSE YOUR HUMANITY

"Most companies that go through layoffs are never the same. They don't recover because trust is broken."

–Ben Horowtiz, Co-Founder of
Andreesen Horowitz

A s 2022 came to a close, the decades-long sweetheart journey of many of Silicon Valley's most championed companies began to head in an entirely new direction – down, way down.

The profit-packing bite had finally come out of the FANG stocks (as Facebook, Amazon, Netflix, Google were referred to at the time). By the time the tumultuous 2022 year came to an end, Mark Zuckerberg's personal net worth had collapsed by more than half as the founder of Facebook (now Meta) shed $60 billion in personal wealth. Twitter underwent one of the most volatile public corporate takeovers in American history and then subsequently laid off half of its workforce even before its "X" identity crisis. Netflix which had been the darling of the COVID era, ended the third quarter with its stock cut in half.

There was a palpable feeling of dread throughout the Valley as Wall Street embraced a new yardstick for measuring success: profitability. No longer worshiping at the altar of growth at all costs, Wall Street's appetite in a post-COVID world had shifted to revenue and profits.

Against this backdrop the once high-flying tech industry was thrust into an unprecedented slew of layoff announcements. Meta announced it would lay off more than 10 percent of its workforce (only to announce another 10 percent reduction six months later), Twitter halved its workforce, and the streaming operating system Roku cut 5 percent of its workforce (and would make two more cuts in the ensuing twelve months).

During a two-year period from 2022 to 2023, more than 420,000 well-paid, highly educated employees at previously impervious companies were walked out the door. The tidal wave of losses in such a condensed period provided a unique time capsule within which to view effective communication strategies for managing what for any leader is one of the most dreaded decisions to make: laying off employees, friends, and colleagues. They have lost their jobs not because of a lack of skill but largely due to the poor planning and execution of the leadership that typically remains unimpacted by the reductions.

Three layoffs, in particular, provide valuable insights into how good managers lead from the front in tough times and, conversely, how a failure to truly plan out the communications strategy of a layoff can make an already painful situation worse for everyone.

Let's start with the bad. In 2022, Better, one of the hottest tech startups in the mortgage lending space which had snagged a $7 billion valuation, had fallen on hard times. The company needed to eliminate hundreds of jobs and made the decision to make these cuts weeks before the holiday season.

I have had to manage communications for several companies looking to make layoffs around the holiday season to recognize the financial benefit on the books before the year-end close. The timing discussion is always gut wrenching and usually comes down to two deciding factors: Do you delay any actions and provide the workforce a blissfully ignorant holiday unaware that the floor is about to drop out from under them, or do you drop the hammer and ruin Christmas?

My counsel to every leader in these tough times has always been, first and foremost, to not lose their humanity. It may seem like a simple reminder, but in times when tough decisions are made that have real-life impacts on those around you it can often be the simplest and most profound guidance. Ask yourself, how would you want to be treated? How would you want your spouse to be treated? I have found when applying this filter that the answer to the question of timing is universal. Time is the single most valuable resource any of us have. And, in a life-altering layoff scenario, providing as much "time" (or notice) to impacted employees to plan for their own future is always the right answer.

One large reduction I helped guide was presented with the kind of "no-win" scenario familiar to any organization that has faced an end of the year layoff: delay notifying the impacted workforce until after the holidays and provide one month severance, or, inform them immediately and provide twice the severance package of two months. When the leadership team put themselves into the shoes of those who would be out of a job, the decision was obvious.

So, the first and most critical lesson from the frontlines of any workforce reduction is to remain human and act humanely. When the company clearly communicated to the entire team why the decision was being announced three weeks before the end of the year (to be able to double the exit packages and provide more time for planning) the blow was substantially softened as everyone—both those impacted and those remaining—felt the company had placed the needs of the employees first.

Because this company never lost its humanity, or the "trust" Ben Horowitz cautioned could be lost in a layoff, it would have the opportunity to expertly navigate its layoff crisis moment. More about the right path in a moment, but first let's return to Better.

Unlike our example above, Better failed to clear the "humanity" hurdle right out of the gate after making the decision to lay off about 10 percent of its workforce.

Gathering a large group together on a Zoom call, CEO Vishal Garg announced without emotion that: "If you're on this call, you are part of the unlucky group that is being laid off. Your employment here is terminated effective immediately."

What started off rocky enough turned into a masterclass of incompetence. Emails attacking the departing employees as being "lazy" would soon surface. Ultimately, the entire communications leadership team would resign in protest of the mangled actions of its management.

Moving into damage control the CEO quickly addressed his mistakes and claimed full responsibility, promising to do better in the future. While this may have set the stage for a rebound opportunity down the line, in the case of Better, things only got worse. Several months after the initial cuts, the company had to conduct a second round of layoffs. Having learned nothing about the need for a detailed communication and HR coordinated plan, the company accidentally deposited the severance benefits into the bank accounts of hundreds of impacted employees before they were notified that they had been laid off. Only by checking their bank accounts did the newly unemployed workers discover they had been shown the door.

While the comedy of errors at Better seem almost impossible to believe, the tone-deaf nature in which they mangled one of the most sensitive times in their employees' lives would play out again and again and again at organizations both big and small in 2022 and 2023. Amazon would be forced to announce the company was laying off more than 18,000 people, but due to planning challenges, the company couldn't tell its workforce who would be impacted for two weeks. Two weeks was an eternity for every single employee being made to worry that their number would come up next. Not only was Amazon going to deliver horrible news eventually to 18,000 employees, but it had also unnecessarily put its entire workforce of nearly two million people through hell. Google sent generic emails to the personal accounts of employees who had been with the company for decades informing them they had been laid off. One employee was so sure it was a phishing scam he didn't believe it until he tried to log on to his work account and found he had been locked out.

In every lay off I have been involved with over the past two decades there has come a moment when the fight between speed and compassion comes to a head. My experience managing layoffs at Fortune 500 public companies, fast growth tech start-ups and even government organizations has highlighted the inarguable truth that there is always time to be humane.

One organization I worked with had to notify a third of its workforce, in a three-hour window that they would be terminated. Rather than send an email or schedule a soulless Zoom call, the executive team divided the list of impacted employees amongst themselves taking the time to either call or meet with each impacted colleague personally. At first, there was fear that these would become soul-sucking meetings of sadness, but I can tell you that the impacted employee on the other end of the conversation was grateful to have a person to talk to immediately, someone who cared for them and held their hand (albeit some virtually) during one of the hardest moments in their careers. What started off as a wrenching experience soon became almost therapeutic for many of those conducting the conversations who were themselves suffering from "survivor's guilt."

A few quick tactical notes are called for here. The goal of these five-minute discussions was not to answer every imaginable question of a rightly frightened newly unemployed former member of the team. In fact, the sheer shock of the news will mean those being informed and consoled will be incapable of registering the right questions that will only come with time and space to reflect on the news. The purpose of these "human" engagements is to make the individual feel valued and appreciated and, importantly, to apologize for the company's inability to retain them. In a layoff, your former colleagues are not being fired for cause. They are being let go because the organization failed to reach a level of performance it had hired for.

There will be time later for HR processing calls, and other efforts that can be managed with more sterile processes. Additionally, initial outreach efforts cannot be focused on just the departed. As we learned from the data breach example earlier, while LinkedIn did a wonderful job communicating to those impacted, they failed to let the other 90 percent of their community know they were not impacted. That silence bread fear and, ultimately, anger. The same rules apply in a layoff. It is critical the survivors hear quickly that they are, in fact, going to be okay.

Showing humanity can take many forms. Perhaps the most illustrative example I have ever witnessed came from

Tim Cadogan, the lively British-American co-founder and CEO of a once fast-growing technology company that had reached the decision no founder ever wants to face. Cadogan needed to lay off about a fifth of his employees, many of whom he had hired personally during his nearly decade-long run leading the business.

In the final planning minutes before announcements were to be made, Cadogan looked at me from across the conference room and said aloud, almost to himself: "Where should I be as people learn the news?" Few leaders in my experience have the emotional EQ Cadogan possesses, so I turned the question back on him. "Where do you want to be?" I asked.

He thought for a moment and said with an audible pang in his voice that he wanted to be able to shake every impacted employee's hand or hug them goodbye personally. This was taking humanity to a super-human level.

Sure enough, as the hour came and meetings were being held, dozens of employees in the headquarters were informed they were being let go. Cadogan stood by the elevator for hours on the main floor, shaking every hand, hugging, sharing stories and tears with those departing. It was one of the most profound experiences I have witnessed in my career. The CEO, the man who was responsible for leading the company, stood at the door and apologized to each person and thanked them for all they had given his company. It was pure and it was raw. Not only did he help bring compassion to those departing, he sent a powerful message to those who would remain that the CEO cared.

This is where the second key lesson of any layoff situation may feel like it comes into conflict with the first (being humane to those departing).

While departing colleagues must be treated with the compassion the situation calls for, the focus must almost immediately shift to the "survivors" – the remaining workforce that will be wracked with guilt, uncertainty, and fear.

The primary goal of any reorganization effort is to pivot from the momentarily dark path currently traveled to a brighter future. To successfully thread this needle will require an engaged workforce believing in the leadership and the mission they had originally signed on to.

Employees will make long lasting judgments about their leadership and the organization they have chosen to be a part of based first on how the dismissals of their friends and colleagues were handled, but then almost immediately will to how they see themselves fitting into the organization's next chapter.

They will need to know quickly that they are okay—that the future ahead is one they would want to stick around for. Knowing that "the worst is behind them" is the most important message to deliver. It is also why, in literally every layoff situation I have advised, I am unequivocally clear that the best approach is to make the deepest cuts necessary in one fell swoop. Rip the Band Aid off and do not allow yourself to fall victim to the "drip, drip, drip" of death by a thousand cuts simply because you "hoped" the numbers would change.

The damage from these multiple rounds cannot be understated. The workforce will no longer believe the worst is behind them and they will no longer trust that their leadership has a handle on the business. Just as the public lost confidence in British Petroleum as they constantly had to restate the amount of oil leaking into the Gulf on an almost daily basis, employees will lose faith that their leadership has a clear understanding of the path ahead.

The third lesson should start to feel familiar at this point. In every crisis, there is a moment when attention is finely attuned to "what you do next." In a layoff, your stakeholder audiences (customers, investors, analysts, employees, voters, whatever they may be) will be looking for signs of life or death. Your immediate public actions will signal whether your efforts have reinvigorated the team with enough gas in the tank for the journey ahead or whether they were simply the final gasps before an inevitably bad ending.

The sooner you engage your external audiences on the future you are building toward, the sooner you can turn the page from the past actions to focus on your new story. Don't "hope for" the opportunity to present itself. You need to plan for it just as deeply as you planned the layoff itself. Be visible. Stand tall and deliver your message from whatever venues you have at your disposal. Meet with reporters. Go on podcasts. Tour your office locations. Speak at industry panels or community events. No matter how hard it may be to shift your own mentality from the pain of the recent past, nothing will show signs of future life more effectively than the bounce in your step and the confidence on your face as you give people a reason to believe again.

CHAPTER 24

RUMSFELD IN THE RING

*"The media's the most powerful entity
on earth. They have the power to make
the innocent guilty and to make the
guilty innocent, and that's power."*

–Malcolm X

N o one in the political arena in the last forty years was more adept at managing the media than Donald H. Rumsfeld. Both America's youngest serving and longest serving secretary of defense (youngest under the Ford Administration and longest serving during his second appointment in the George W. Bush administration), Rumsfeld could teach a graduate course on how to effectively advance a clear message during a crisis.

To understand just how successful Rumsfeld was at managing the pugilistic enterprise of jousting with the media, one needs to go back in time and watch the press briefings during the early days of the Iraq War. I was honored to work for Rumsfeld and be in the back row for many of those magical moments. Networks would break into their daily shows to cover the must-watch press conferences. Reporters would arrive early for front-row seats as random officials and Pentagon guests crammed into the briefing room's back row, packing the walls to watch the "show" that the old master was about to put on.

Having witnessed countless numbers of these briefings and been in the room before, during and after several sessions as a member of Rumsfeld's press team, what struck me the most was the rigid process the SECDEF—as we called him—followed before each encounter. The approach the seasoned Washington hand would take before every press encounter or public engagement provides one of the surest game plans for media relations success anyone could hope to follow.

A half-century before his second tour of duty in Washington in the early 2000s, Rumsfeld had been a stand-out college athlete. But football, basketball, and baseball were not his calling; he was a champion wrestler and captain of the college team at Princeton. Watching Rumsfeld prepare for his new "matches" in the media ring, I was struck by the three phases the wily wrestler would go through before, during and after each encounter to ensure he came out on top.

Pre-Match

Here is where the first lesson about how to manage a press briefing is learned. Wrestling is not a team sport; it is one of the purest forms of gladiatorial combat remaining today. Its goal is simple. There can be only one winner and one loser.

To win, one must pin the opponent into submission. There are no timeouts. No instant replays. There is only an arena, a mat, two opponents, and a desire to win.

The pre-match Rumsfeld was a sponge. He wanted every bit of available information. He absorbed every military briefing, combat report, and foreign policy update with a near encyclopedic mind. He asked penetrating questions. He wanted to know more about every possible question than his opponent did. Speaking several months after Rumsfeld retired from the Pentagon, a senior military commander said that when you briefed the Secretary, you had to be on your best game because he typically knew your job as well as you did. In 2021, when many of us gathered for his funeral at Arlington, eulogist Vice President Dick Cheney and former chairman of the Joint Chiefs of Staff Dick Meyers all repeated this refrain.

Rummy came prepared. No surprises. He was ready to answer every question that came his way, but also, and most importantly, to deliver the message he came to deliver. He was not going into the arena simply to get batted around. He was not coming to play the media's game. He was coming to win. When the pull to "get in front of the story" lands you in front of the hot lights of the media, be sure you came to play. Have a clear story ready to be told. Too often I hear from those in crisis that we have to "respond to the questions coming in." That is a sure-fire recipe for failure. This is your match. You set the rules and you come with the moves you want to deliver. Any questions you answer are on your terms, with your messaging and focus.

In the Match

The second phase of Rumsfeld's press engagement strategy is what I call the "in the match" Rumsfeld. Eyes locked, the seventy-something bespectacled Secretary of Defense was a steely fox. While only 5'7, he commanded the lectern and entered the ring guided by several key principles that shaped his outlook on the craft. These principles could apply just as well to military troop movements as they do to anyone preparing to enter a hostile media environment. Rumsfeld himself outlined these principles in his book *Rumsfeld's Rules: Leadership Lessons in Business, Politics, War, and Life*

Rule #1: "Be precise. A lack of precision is dangerous when the margin of error is small."

This point is critical and speaks to lessons from previous chapters on British Petroleum and others who failed to deliver laser-like precision during their media engagement. The crisis annals are replete with examples of those who allowed themselves to be tugged off course, pulled away from addressing only what they knew they knew (their "known knowns," to paraphrase Rumsfeld) toward the hazardous territory of what they did not know.

When one faces the media, they must recognize they are in the arena. There is an expected give and take. Your job is to stay in your lane, stick to your playbook and win. You don't get brownie points for trying to answer a reporter's question that you don't know the answer to (or that you are not ready to address). Be precise and stick to your game plan. You have a message to deliver and if that is all anyone hears—you win.

Rule #2: "Learn to say, 'I don't know.' If used when appropriate, it will be often."

Time and again, the initial information received amid a crisis is incomplete or highly likely to change as the hours and days unfold. Rather than guess, own your lack of visibility and embrace your imperfections. Let the reporter know what you do not know and that you are as eager to discover the answers as they are. You will gain credibility for being transparent and, most importantly, you will not risk losing whatever reputational or moral authority you have left by being wrong.

Rule #3: "If you foul up, correct it fast. Delay only compounds mistakes."

Mistakes are bound to happen in your crisis response. The sooner you accept this, the sooner you can get over it. Information will change. What you believed to be true will be proven wrong. The scope of your crisis will be much bigger than anticipated, either in those it affects or in the cost to repair the damage or any other litany of "unknown unknowns" that come your way.

The hardest moments in my career spent managing crisis response efforts have always come when an apology for a mistaken comment or past fact was needed. It is astonishing how hard it is for many to utter those three little words: "I was wrong." It is equally surprising how powerful they remain today. The public loves contrition. They love the humanizing effect of someone in power recognizing they made a mistake and owning it. Lawyers will fight tooth and nail to strip any semblance of acknowledgment of wrongdoing away, but it is the responsibility of a leader in a time of crisis to own the mistakes, big and small. If the information you delivered has shifted, own it quickly before others discover it. Share with the public that the objective was an overriding desire to push out information as soon as possible in the most transparent way and, as the crisis has unfolded, new information has come to light. Don't delay. As Rumsfeld noted, it will only compound the mistakes and could make what should appear as an honest incorrect statement look like an attempt to deliberately mislead the public.

Rule #4: "Don't divide the world into 'them' and 'us.' Avoid infatuation with or resentment of the press... they have their jobs and you have yours."

Just as a wrestler shakes the hand of an opponent before a match, recognize that both sides in an interview have an important job to do. This will significantly smooth out press engagements as animosity and other emotional baggage get checked at the door. In a crisis, it will be natural to vilify the media. "How dare they say that about me" may be the first thought in your mind. You will be hurt personally and professionally. You will want to extract a pound of flesh from the reporters. Your attitude, your tone, your very demeanor, will set the stage for how the match unfolds. Rumsfeld's lesson here is less about preparation and more about presentation—the attitude you carry into the ring. To be sure, the reporter sitting across from you is not your friend. Nor will they be after this crisis. But they don't have to be your enemy either.

Rumsfeld knew this better than most and built a begrudging shared respect with the media for the job each had to do. That is not to say he came ready to fight to a draw. He still came to each match prepared to win totally, to pin his opponent into submission and win the day. He just did it with a smile, a joke, and an occasional zinger to establish in the beginning that he was in charge of the briefing and that he respected the opponent he was about to square off against.

As I think back to my time on Rumsfeld's staff, I think this is one of the key lessons I took away that has helped me build strong relationships with the media I work with. Both before and during a crisis, it is important to remember that the media is not the enemy. The old adage of catching more flies with honey is true far more times than not, even in a potentially adversarial relationship.

During a lecture some years back, I was challenged on this point. A graduate student suggested that the die was already cast in a crisis for the press to be adversarial and that there was little hope of building a trusting relationship. As I hear such comments, I am always reminded of a trip I took in 2005 to the detention facility in Guantanamo Bay, Cuba. At the time, I led outreach efforts for the Pentagon's office charged with engaging with military media analysts and keeping them informed about the ongoing wars in Iraq and

Afghanistan. On this trip along with about a dozen analysts, we were working to combat false perceptions of broken-down detention centers (the new facility at GITMO had just been rated better than nearly every prison in the US) and address false perceptions of ongoing interrogation tactics. As we cleared the briefing room and proceeded to watch an active interrogation underway, I was stunned by what I saw.

On the other side of the glass, I watched a US interrogator hand a magazine and a candy bar to a terrorist insurgent who had American blood on his hands. The two were having a normal chat—had the location been different, you could imagine the exact same conversation occurring at your local coffee shop. As the interrogation concluded and we had the opportunity to speak to the officer in charge, I asked about what we had just seen. "You catch more flies with honey," said the seasoned officer. Even in this situation, where enemies could not more starkly be set in opposition to each other, the adversarial relationship didn't have to be disrespectful. In fact, the officer made it clear that it wouldn't benefit his cause for it to be so. By building relationships and trust, doors open and even the slightest bits of information can slip through. The same is true for your crisis media relations. Despite how it may feel when you're being grilled under the hot media lights, reporters are humans too. They have a job to do and it is to cover your crisis. But, by having the conversations that build trust, opportunities are created to smooth the edges of a story or glean important insights ahead of time.

Whenever possible, take the time to know the reporters covering your space and become a trusted resource not just for information about you or your organization or cause, but for broader thought leadership ahead of time. Host an annual "off the record" roundtable with the top reporters who cover your space to have "face time" with those writing about you. Personalize your story and invest in the relationship ahead of time. Take them out for coffee or a beer without any agenda other than "getting to know" one another. I have found in my career that many of the best relationships I have built over the years are with the reporters I have been lucky enough to work with. They are bright, passionate storytellers who care deeply for their craft and for the truth. By building trust now, you will have built a reservoir of credibility and goodwill to draw upon when the critical questions come.

After the Match

I mentioned there were three phases of any Rumsfeld press briefing. The first two have been covered, the pre-match learning phase and the in-the-ring gladiator phase. The last phase, the post-match, towel snapping, jovial Rumsfeld, was always the most fun to witness. Rumsfeld had a hilarious sense of humor and an impish smile that drew people into his orbit. Even in the toughest times, he had the perspective to know he needed to laugh, if for no other reason than to give his team a moment to relax. And after he had won, he was always a gracious sport with reporters.

In 2003, Rumsfeld faced stinging criticism in the press for a memo he circulated to senior leaders at the Pentagon outlining the many possible challenges the United States faced in Iraq and Afghanistan. In the memo—we called such memos "snowflakes" because so many fell from his pen it was like snowing sheets of paper—Rumsfeld cautioned that the United States faced a potentially "long, hard slog" in the war on terrorism. On October 23, 2003, *The New York Times* reported on Rumsfeld's interaction with the media concerning the memo, which highlighted his approach to media relations. According to the *Times*, "Mr. Rumsfeld, primarily addressing the memo, made an effort today to defuse the criticism with humor. He cited a definition of 'slog' that emphasized hitting an enemy hard. Asked about a more traditional definition that emphasized slow and messy going, he smiled and said: "I read the one I liked."

In any crisis situation, it is important to find the time to embrace the small wins and to recognize a task done well while taking a moment to breathe. You may not be all the way through the crisis thicket; in fact, your darkest hours may still lie ahead. However, you and your team cannot remain on a hair trigger for days and weeks on end. Recognize the points you put on the board and regroup for the next match that may be hours or minutes away. When the next bell sounds off, get back into the ring ready to win again.

A Princely Mess

One final example from 2019 provides a compelling book-end case study on the importance of having an actual game plan for engaging the press, rather than just "showing up" to be batted around.

In a December 2019 article for *Forbes* titled "A Royal Mess: Lessons in Crisis Communications from Prince Andrew's BBC Interview," Evan Nierman, founder and CEO of Red Banyan, a strategic PR and crisis communications firm, provides an insightful analysis of how the Duke of York violated every single one of Rumsfeld's rules. Nierman writes:

> Facing accusations of sexual misconduct and growing scrutiny of his close friendship with convicted sexual predator Jeffrey Epstein, Prince Andrew decided to step out in front of the cameras to address the allegations head-on. The result was a public image debacle that ticked every box for what a person in crisis should strenuously avoid in a live TV interview. The prince's likely hope for the interview was to reassure the public of his innocence and clear up any lingering questions about his friendship with Epstein, but his performance invited even *more* speculation. Now, he finds himself at the very center of controversy, looking worse than ever before.

This is the downside that can come from a desire to simply "get in front of the cameras" without a strategy and without being totally unprepared to win. As Nierman sums up in his post,

> Prince Andrew began turning his public crisis from bad to worse. With shifting eyes, a

needlessly defensive posture and tonality and haphazard attempts to "set the story straight" through a shaky version of events, it became painfully obvious that he was wholly unprepared for the interview...setting aside the unconvincing demeanor and poor optics surrounding his appearance, the prince's words themselves also did little toward establishing credibility. Parts of the interview were nearly indistinguishable from a comedy sketch mocking a hapless interview. He gave inexplicable, rambling answers to serious allegations being made against him by his accuser. He also cornered himself by making definitive statements on a situation that is still evolving.

Prince Andrew's media debacle will serve for years as a textbook example of an engagement that was doomed to failure before the cameras ever began rolling. The Duke of York had no plan for success. His public relations advisor resigned in protest before the interview. He had laughable excuses for what should have been easily anticipated, and prepared for, questions. From his mysterious medical condition that made it impossible for him to "sweat" to his suggestion that photos of him had been doctored, with each new comment the hole he dug for himself became ever deeper.

As Nierman concluded in his column: "Rather than delivering pithy, credible soundbites, the prince served up incoherent explanations that would have been laughable had they not been related to the deadly serious issue of sexual misconduct. A strong set of talking points would have gone a long way toward helping him avoid such a pitiful performance.… Professional PR preparation cannot be neglected, and as Prince Andrew learned the hard way, a 'no sweat' approach to crisis management can lead to a royal headache."

The most important lesson from Prince Andrew's train wreck is that he did not appear to have had a "purpose" for being there to begin with, other than to swing at pitch after pitch tossed his way. This defensive strategy could have only one outcome. As Rumsfeld once said during a briefing, "Defense is for losers." In this case, he was right again.

When a crisis media engagement comes for you, recognize at once where you are: on the mat, preparing to wrestle out your truth. Stay calm, get ready, and remain in control.

CHAPTER 25

YOUR SECRET WEAPON IS SITTING RIGHT NEXT TO YOU

*"If you take care of your employees,
they will take care of your business."*

–Sir Richard Branson

n Chapter 7, the importance of training employees to understand the new rules of engagement in today's digital world of reputation management was on full display with our young Israeli military officer whose poor judgment on social media nearly caused an international fire storm. It could be easy to take away from this and other case studies that employees should be seen as a risk to be mitigated in a crisis. The truth, however, paints a far more inclusive picture. While many crises have been catalyzed unintentionally by employees who simply "didn't know better," it is also true that in many instances, employees themselves carry the greatest potential to put out your crisis fires.

Think for a moment about this question: In a crisis, who has the most to gain from successfully navigating the turbulent waters that threaten to capsize your organizational boat? Investors? Sure, but they have lots of other boats in the sea. Customers? Maybe, but again unless you have unlocked the secret of aging or found the cure to cancer, they will likely find a replacement for your goods or services in rather quick order. The answer is likely sitting right next to you. You see them every day in the copy room, on Zoom calls and in the parking lot. Your co-workers have more to gain than anyone—and more to lose—from the outcome of your crisis situation. If for no other reason than the fact that their paycheck could be on the line, engaged and passionate employees can become the most effective advocates in your network. While this fact may seem obvious, what is less obvious to many is how best to mobilize and deploy in-house foot soldiers when a crisis actually occurs.

In a study published in the Journal of Public Relations, Korean researchers Dr. Jeong-Nam Kim and Dr. Yunna Rhee defined the three key roles employees can play in a crisis: megaphoning, scouting, and micro-boundary spanning. While the researchers applied nifty terminology to each, they are in essence very basic steps any organization can take to leverage their workforce for good in a crisis.

Megaphoning

In the megaphoning role, employees voluntarily share both internal and external positive information about their employer with their network of friends and relatives. Consider your own behavior patterns when you see something critical on the news. How often do you turn to social media or your private friend text group to ask others for their opinions on the topic? And, if one of your connections happens to have "inside information," how likely are you to give even greater weight to those stories than to others you may have heard from the news?

In its 2021 Trust Barometer, global public relations agency Edelman released its most damning report on trust overall. Trust in "media" had dropped to a flatline of only 50 percent. While trust in "my local community" was nearly 20 basis points higher. With the proliferation of partisan media channels and the flood of fake news, many simply turn to those closest to them in a crisis as the most trusted source for information. Leveraging the employee megaphone in a crisis can rapidly amplify your messaging and instill much-needed credibility at the "grassroots" level.

I have four personal favorite tools for helping employees megaphone for the company.

Internal Email

First, again think about how you receive information and how you validate it. Are you more likely to trust a press release you read from a company or an "internal email" sent from the CEO to the workforce? We are all human and our instincts are to trust the insider note as being more raw—more real and less polished—than the slick PR statement. In a crisis, use this to your advantage. Email your workforce the facts about what is happening in a format you fully expect will be reposted, shared, or quoted. Your team members will be asked by their friends and family and neighbors what is going on. Your email provides them the tools to share "information from our CEO on what is happening." You have armed them with the script for their megaphone without ever having to ask for their support.

Video

Another great resource is video. In a crisis, consider posting an internal video with your organization's messaging directly to your workforce. Expect this content to be shared widely. Expect your team members to post to their social sites that "they just heard from the CEO on a video and he/she said x or y."

Meeting

Third, consider the employee all-hands conference call or Zoom meeting to quickly engage your workforce with the facts and show your team that you are standing against the crisis—standing up for them—and you are thankful for their help. This motivational moment will further amplify the megaphone.

Social Media

Finally, don't forget the obvious fact that your employees are all on social media. Develop messaging they can easily repurpose to reach their own social networks. LinkedIn posts from a CEO, a YouTube video posted externally, or a tweet that links to a blog post provides easy ammunition for your workforce to repurpose and deploy on your behalf without having to take a "position." Asking your employees to defend the company to their friends and family is never easy and rarely recommended. Instead, by putting the information out there, readily available to share, you are creating the environment where an employee can, if they choose, become an apostle for the organization in times of crisis.

Scouting

In Kim and Rhee's second role, that of scouting, employees assume the role of information gatherer or "scout," bringing critical information back to the organization that it may have missed. With so much information happening today—literally millions of videos, blogs, tweets, and snaps posting every minute—no organization can capture the totality of what is being said about them daily. This reality is only compounded in a crisis when the volume of content accelerates exponentially. Having employee lines of communication open that not only allow for, but encourage, the free flow of information up the chain on potential crises can serve as both an early warning system as well as a great force multiplier for your monitoring services.

To equip your employees with the tools for scouting, consider the following options.

Hotlines

Establish a unique email address or portal that can serve as a hotline where employees can send information that might be valuable and could help the company respond to the crisis. Ask a few trusted employees to regularly vet this input for information that will be critical in aiding your crisis response efforts and empower them to carry it up the chain of command.

Internal Collaboration Tools:

Many organizations today deploy internal collaboration tools such as Slack to help foster the sharing of real-time intelligence. One company I was affiliated with had more than 1,000 Slack channels. Some were very focused on an immediate crisis, while others were more broadly established for information-sharing on competitive intelligence. The ability to rapidly drop a link or a note into a channel to help feed the broader understanding has a way of becoming addictive. Employees feel a need to "share what they are hearing" and thus almost subconsciously begin listening carefully for insights they can bring back to the collective.

Micro-boundary Spanning

The final role of "micro-boundary spanning," while a little over the top in its phrasing, is simply the combination of megaphoning and scouting. When you combine these two disciplines, you have truly turned employees from paycheck gatherers to fans and ultimately into apostles who are invested in the organizational reputation and prepared to take the good message forward.

CHAPTER 26

EMERGING VICTORIOUS

"The Chinese use two brush strokes to write the word 'crisis.' One brush stroke stands for danger; the other for opportunity. In a crisis, be aware of the danger—but recognize the opportunity."

–John F. Kennedy

In times of crisis, one of the hardest concepts to grasp is the reality that there will be better days ahead. To be sure, this is not always the case. Sometimes, a crisis is so devastating it cannot be overcome. Companies collapse (think Arthur Andersen following the Enron scandal). But even in those times, there are opportunities for rebirth. While Arthur Andersen ceased to exist, from out of its ashes arose Accenture, which in 2024 boasted a global workforce of more than half a million people and a market cap of nearly a quarter trillion dollars.

In times of crisis, you must focus on the immediate fire raging, but be mindful of the ancient Chinese proverb and stay alert for the opportunity hidden within. In nearly every crisis I have faced in my career, there is a moment in time, a small moment and one that can be missed, where the crisis waters have subsided while the media and the public are still paying full attention to an organization's response efforts.

With so much news today, we often move from one sensational headline to the next with the attention span of a toddler. This moment is exceptionally fleeting, but more often than not, a door will open.

This was the moment Starbucks seized upon in Philadelphia and changed the narrative about how they would approach race relations as a company. As the smoke begins to settle from your extinguished crisis fire, watch for the moment to switch the narrative and leave your stakeholder audiences with a lasting new impression that allows you to rewrite the next chapter of the playbook and make some lemonade from the crisis lemons.

In 2011, as it faced a continued onslaught from the left-leaning Environmental Working Group over the safety of the ingredients in its products, Johnson & Johnson once again found its opportunity in crisis. Every year, the EWG would launch an assault on companies within the personal care products market for what they believed were unsafe chemicals inside many of the most popular products used by consumers today. Everything from toothpaste to shampoo was on the radar of this activist group. Unfortunately for J&J, as one of the biggest and most well-known players in the market, the EWG aimed much of its fire at the company to maximize media interest and consumer outcry. Attacking smaller companies for far worse actions may seem like the logical approach to take, but those efforts would not attract substantial media attention. And media is the life blood of activist groups that feed on the news cycle to bring in new donors to fund their activities.

Millions of parents were bathing their children each night with Johnson & Johnson's Baby Shampoo, and if the activists could spook parents, they could drive a strong media cycle.

J&J had decades of safety studies and hundreds of the best scientists, nurses, and other parent leaders working on the development of its products. Yet they recognized that this debate over "ingredient safety" was not going to be won by simply explaining the science. J&J knew all too well the old crisis adage, "if you are explaining you are losing," and they knew instinctively this fight was not going to be won on the merits of science.

The EWG was using the boogie man of the "unknown" against the entire personal care industry. For the past century, it had been common practice for most companies to not list the ingredients of their products on the label. It was not required, and most companies considered their ingredient list a trade secret. The EWG used this lack of transparency to feed controversy where none really needed to exist. EWG was a dog with a bone when it came to Johnson & Johnson, and the company knew it. They needed to change the game and introduce an entirely new playbook.

After years of fighting against the baseless attacks, we recognized an opportunity to reposition J&J as the first in the industry to fully embrace transparency, co-opting the EWG's messaging and creating a marketing opportunity to drive even greater sales.

At the same time, the company could refocus attention and pressure on competitors. J&J leaned into their crisis, finding the opportunity and ultimately releasing all their ingredients. The unthinkable happened next. The president of the EWG embraced the opportunity to now grab even greater media attention by *praising* J&J. The activist group that only months earlier had worked to scare parents about the company's products was now praising J&J for their "transparency" and their "commitment" to consumers and for "raising the industry bar." A decade later, in 2020, J&J was again named the most trusted and valued pharmaceutical brand in the business.

Not every crisis will have a clear moment to switch the narrative. But nearly every crisis will have an opening. Domino's found its moment and used the searing lights of crisis to reframe its entire business around quality and, in the process, innovated an entirely new menu and a new technology enabling customers to track their pizza's progress from the oven to the door. This commitment grew the company stock more than 6,000 percent from the midst of the crisis in 2009 to its all-time high in 2021. Sometimes, the light at the end of the tunnel is not a train barreling down upon you—it just might be the opportunity you have been waiting for.

CHAPTER 27
WHEN CRISIS COMES HOME

"This is evolving science. You are seeing sausages being made—in front of the world's eyes."

– Saad Omer, epidemiologist and
Yale vaccine researcher

n 2012, my family and I moved from Washington, DC, to settle into a new life in Southern California. We moved into a suburb about thirty minutes outside of Los Angeles, nestled in the rolling foothills of the Santa Monica mountains. The mountains surrounding our little town provided both a physical barrier, and a mental one, from the big city life.

Not long after our arrival, I had the opportunity to run for public office, seeking an open seat on our school district's board of education.

After a competitive campaign across the four cities and two counties our schools serviced, I emerged victorious and set out on a journey that would lead me through some of the most intense crisis moments of my career—responding to ravaging wildfires, forced evacuations, union fights, school safety after the Parkland shooting, and, of course, the COVID-19 pandemic.

At each turn during these crisis moments, I was struck by how few in public life really understood effective communications. This time in public service also reminded me of how much I have benefited from the lifetime of lessons covered in this book.

One weekend, as I prepared to complete this manuscript, I was introduced to a superbly fun new Netflix original show, *Cobra Kai*, the modern-day streaming reboot of the *Karate Kid* movie franchise.

Watching the program was a nostalgic trip down memory lane for an eighties kid like me, yet it also seemed to provide a perfect reference point and concluding chapter for a book designed to build within each of us the instincts to anticipate risk and respond accordingly.

In the show's second season, viewers were reintroduced to the classic lessons of "wax on, wax off," "paint the fence," and "clean the windows," as Ralph Macchio's Daniel LaRusso trains a new generation of karate students.

As any *Karate Kid* fan can tell you, the purpose from the countless hours of waxing cars and painting fence posts was to build an instinctive muscle memory for how one should react in certain rapid-fire instances. Watching *Cobra Kai* made me think about the "muscle memory" I had gained from waxing and painting through the crisis trenches of my career.

At some point for every crisis manager, the crisis will come home, and with it will come an opportunity to move from counselor to the actual individual at the center of the storm. It is in these instances that you really discover whether the lessons learned guiding others instilled the instinctive memory necessary for your own survival.

Putting Lessons into Practice

In the immediate aftermath of 2018's Parkland shooting that left seventeen dead in Florida, I was serving as the president of the Board of Education. The parents of our 10,000+ students were rightly terrified. If it could happen in Parkland, many feared, it could happen anywhere.

Several months after the Parkland shooting, the horror and the bloodshed from America's ongoing war with guns would come directly to our community with the mass shooting at the Borderline country music bar in Thousand Oaks, California, which left a dozen people dead. Our community was on edge.

Parents didn't feel safe sending their children to school. As a parent of three young children myself at the time, I understood instinctively the fear that was gripping our community. I also understood the need many felt to be "heard."

In a crisis moment when emotions are running high, similar to elements of cancel culture and other highly emotional breakpoints, you must first listen before you have permission to develop actual solutions. The very act of being heard is a pressure release valve for many. In these situations, your audience simply cannot hear what you have to say until they feel as if they have been heard.

I began a listening tour attending parent association meetings and community gatherings. The irrational fear of the "unknown" was paralyzing many across our district. Looking to the lessons from the past, what was becoming clear was that the unknown—whether our schools were safe—was trumping all other considerations.

Parents and teachers and even students were not looking for a guarantee that a crazed gunman would never come to our campuses. What they wanted to know was whether we had taken every precaution possible to mitigate that moment from ever happening. In other words, the public needed to know—they needed to *feel*—that we had confidence in our knowledge of the situation at hand.

This instinctive human reaction is the same dynamic that has played out in food recalls or other disasters, such as the BP Deepwater Horizon oil leak in the Gulf of Mexico. The public's anxiety only begins to subside not when the problem is definitively solved, but once the public believes that the key issues are understood.

When the public learns that retailers have identified the source of the food-born bacteria in the infected meat, they immediately relax, assuming that, with the unknown out of the way, retailers will have an effective plan for replacing the beef. When an ecommerce site discovers the source of the data breach, the public assumes they will find a way to close it off and make it right. The daily re-evaluation of the BP disaster highlighted to the public that the oil giant really had no idea what was going on, and this uncertainty fueled anxiety of the unknown. If they couldn't determine how bad the oil leak was day to day, then surely, most thought, they have no idea how to fix it.

As we moved our community from the fear stage to the action stage, again, the muscle memory kicked in. Now that we were listening as a school district, the public was willing to hear what actions we would take next. Recognizing the value of third-party validation and of independent expertise, we hired one of the nation's foremost experts on campus safety to conduct a complete audit of every campus. In this instance, it was critical to lean on independent, outside credibility. Just as the data breach victim wants to remind the public that they are working hand in hand with law enforcement as a powerful third-party validator, our effort needed that additional thrust of support. Our consultant was a regular advisor to the FBI, which lent an extra layer of expertise and credibility.

The campus safety teams we had assembled reviewed every site, speaking with teachers and parents and ultimately delivering a confidential report to our board. Here, once again, our community reacted as one would expect. Knowing that an expert had been contracted, and that a list of recommendations had been delivered, the community relaxed further. Not a single new policy had been adopted yet. However, the very fact that we had undertaken the process provided enough currency that most believed any necessary steps would be taken.

As we exited the darkest hours of the gun safety debate, we then took the next step to leverage the crisis cycle to our advantage. While the community was watching to see what we did next, we rolled out a series of highly visible new safety protocols including new fencing, cameras, and state-of-the-art campus badging systems. The community could not only see the actions being taken with new physical barriers and protocols, they could also "feel" these changes go into effect.

At each step of the way, we communicated. We developed videos on campus safety and new badging procedures. We met with parents and teachers. We never let the vacuum of silence overtake the discussion and we never hesitated. Several months after the events of Parkland and our response, I would stand for re-election in a community that only months earlier was on a knife's edge. I would receive the most votes of my career. And, a few years later, the entire community would vote to pass a quarter billion-dollar bond supporting the schools with many calling out our commitment to student safety as a key benchmark for their support.

With the lessons of 2018 firmly established in our collective muscle memory, I believed we were likely ready for any crisis as a district. We would face massive fires and evacuations in the ensuring years and budget woes and union fights. However, nothing prepared us for the unprecedented nature of COVID-19. It would stretch and test every norm of public education and crisis communications as it put local elected school leaders at the center of some of the most contentious and hotly debated topics in the history of our country.

Coping with Contagion

From school masking requirements to mandatory teacher and student vaccinations, we had never seen anything like the level of anger and fear that gripped the national discourse on public education in 2021.

The divide was real. During the spring of 2021, parents on one side of the community were comparing mask requirements to the systemic annihilation of the Jewish people during the Holocaust while parents on the other side of the debate were claiming publicly that if we did not "require mandatory vaccinations of all students, the blood of dead children will be on our hands." The chasm between viewpoints seemed almost insurmountable.

At the same time, federal and state authorities seemed to be constantly out of alignment. Seemingly every day, new and often conflicting state, federal, and local regulations governing masking and vaccinations and school re-openings were flooding into the system. Everyone in the community was an overnight medical expert, quoting blogs or the pandemic "experts" they had seen on their favorite partisan news channel.

School board members in other communities were being harassed. Politicizing local schools helped the insurgent campaign of Glen Youngkin, a first-time politician in Virginia, win an upset gubernatorial election. The same kind of fear that had gripped our community over school shootings had, in the case of COID, transitioned to anger.

Even amid a once-in-a-century global pandemic, however, the crisis fire was burning in expected ways. Misinformation left unaddressed took on the currency of truth.

Shifting priorities on masking, lack of clarity on who would be required to be vaccinated and when students could return to the classroom bred a feeling of uncertainty—a feeling that the school district didn't have a plan. The fear that we didn't "have a plan" and thus must not know what is going on was driving greater angst than the actual positivity rates in our community.

Once again, we leaned into our crisis toolkit. I joined with other board members at local community protests to speak out and share the word about our plans. I aggressively engaged in social media groups that had been formed to help direct parents to the best possible resources. And, importantly, we enlisted the help of parents. As has been discussed in previous chapters, it was critical that our district and our teachers and staff be seen as the victims of COVID and the evolving regulations we were required to follow, and not the villainous mask police making parents' lives hell with endless hours of virtual education, falling grades, and rising mental health concerns.

By enlisting parents to help lobby state and county officials to "let us open our schools," it became clear that we were not the obstacle, but a partner fighting hard to achieve the same goals as our parents. We sent out regular emails with updates. We were active on social media. We lobbied our legislators and county officials. We embraced the mantra of "over-communicating" with a simple message—we want our schools to open, too. We hosted the first community vaccination clinics on our school sites as a vivid sign of our commitment to action. We were one of the first to require our teachers be vaccinated—another clear sign to our parents that we were doing everything we could to open. And, when the opportunity presented itself, we became the very first district in the entire region to re-open all our elementary schools.

To be sure, everything didn't go smoothly. The negative impacts from the "lost year of Zoom" will be with us for a long time. Student mental health is at a crossroads. The risk of suicides and self-harm are at all-time highs. Many students who were already struggling academically before the pandemic collapsed under the pressure of distance learning.

And, while our community fared better than many from the political divisions of COVID, we were not immune from the destructive nature of divisiveness. However, as I hope the lessons in this book have laid out, by holding true to a few core practices, I was able to advocate for my beliefs as we rallied large portions of our community to support common sense safety protocols and the opening of our schools.

In 2022 I once again stood for election, and just as before, I won re-lection with more votes than I had ever received previously.

PARTING THOUGHTS AND ACKNOWLEDGMENTS

W ell, we have come to the end. At least, the end of this part of the crisis journey. After reading through 50,000 words bearing forth a life of experiences in the crisis trenches, it is my hope that you are now armed with the mindset and knowledge to successfully navigate your own crisis fires and emerge stronger than before.

While that may seem like a lofty goal, especially if you have picked up this book in the middle of your own brewing crisis, I can tell you that it is not only possible, it is also largely within your control.

"Crisis craves structure," as an old mentor friend of mine is fond of saying, and hopefully you now feel empowered to bring your own structure together, both during peacetime and in times of crisis.

As you think through the challenges you are facing today, and the concerns or risks you see in the future, I would love to hear your thoughts on how *Communicating Under Fire* impacted your mindset to be crisis ready. I hope you will reach out to me on X (formerly Twitter @dallaslawrence) and share your feedback from your own crisis firefighting tales.

No one has every answer upfront. And, even the most seasoned crisis guides stumble along the way. As the past chapters have detailed, it is not the stumble that matters most, it is what you do next that determines the outcome of the trial you are facing. When armed with the right mindset to engage with tenacious vigor, the outcomes are far more likely to be in your favor.

Taking on the challenge of writing any book cannot be done without the help and support of many people. My experience bringing together *Communicating Under Fire* is no exception. I have been blessed throughout my career to have had incredible mentors who encouraged me to find my voice as I worked my way through the trenches, honing my crisis management experience. From the political arena and the front lines of the war on terror, to some of the biggest corporate crises in the world, these incredible men and women who blazed a trail ahead and alongside of me took the time to bring me along for the ride of a lifetime and I will forever be grateful for their confidence. First and foremost, I must thank the late Harold Burson, the public relations legend who, through tenacity and brilliance, helped shape the field of crisis communications today more than any other leader. Working alongside Harold was one of the highest honors of my career and every communication practitioner owes him a debt of gratitude for the industry he helped create.

I also want to thank Pat Ford, whose leadership example reminded me every day of the importance of truly understanding the values we work to protect; Karen Hughes, whose effortless brilliance is sought out by nearly every world leader and corporate executive; Karen Doyne, with whom I was honored to serve with and learn from in many of the biggest corporate crisis trenches of the early 2000s; Richard Levick and Gene Grabowski, who recognized early the need to think differently about crisis and challenged me to build one of the first "digital crisis" practice groups in the industry; Allison Barber, whose advice and mentorship has helped guide me throughout my career; Karen Dowdy, who gave a young college kid the opportunity to manage his first political campaign; and Kristin Hueter, who taught me some of the most valuable life lessons of my career and whose confidence in my young abilities helped lead me to Washington, DC, and open the door to every significant work experience of my life.

I also must call out the incredible group of people whom I served with in Iraq. Our "Iraq Pack" as we called ourselves has continued to be a wonderful source of joy and inspiration in my life. I am grateful to be Baghdad buddies for life with Susan Phalen, Traci Scott, Sam Whitfield, Alan Davidson, Kristi Clemens Rogers, Pepper Bryars, Joe Pally, Dan Senor, Beth Marple, Shane Wolfe, and Rob Tappen.

After a career spent sitting in war rooms and on the front lines of many global crisis moments, I have learned so much from the colleagues who stood alongside me in those darkest of hours or who helped open new doors to hone my communications skills. To Roxanne Taylor, Alex Pachetti, Dave Bartlett, Jay Leveton, Mark Penn, Karen Johnson, Ashwin Navin, and Scott Rosenberg I offer my sincerest appreciation for a lifetime of lessons you each helped me to learn that could fill entire volumes.

On a more personal note, I also must thank Diane Edwards, my high school speech and debate teacher, who instilled in me the incredible importance of knowing, valuing, and respecting the arguments of both sides of every issue. Every student in America should be lucky enough to have had a Diane Edwards in their corner.

Finally, I would like to thank my wonderful family. My mother, Cathy, who raised me as a single parent while putting herself through college during her lunch breaks to ensure she was always there for her son knows more about surviving crises than anyone I have ever met. And lastly, but certainly not least, I owe a huge debt of gratitude to my incredible wife, Sarah and our amazing kids Emma, Abby, and Christopher for allowing me to go on so many of these crazy crisis rollercoaster rides. With their love, no crisis has ever seemed insurmountable.

ABOUT THE AUTHOR

Dallas Lawrence brings a unique perspective to the crisis management field, having served in the highest levels of the political, government, and corporate worlds. He has taught as an adjunct instructor at the University of Southern California's Annenberg School for Communication, where he developed the graduate course in crisis communications. Dallas's work has earned him multiple honors including Corporate Communicator of the Year, Crisis Manager of the Year, Digital Strategist of the Year, and being named one of the 40 Most Influential Leaders in Public Relations.